Modern Architecture: A Very Short Introduction

VERY SHORT INTRODUCTIONS are for anyone wanting a stimulating and accessible way into a new subject. They are written by experts, and have been translated into more than 45 different languages.

The series began in 1995, and now covers a wide variety of topics in every discipline. The VSI library currently contains over 550 volumes—a Very Short Introduction to everything from Psychology and Philosophy of Science to American History and Relativity—and continues to grow in every subject area.

Very Short Introductions available now:

ABOLITIONISM Richard S. Newman
ACCOUNTING Christopher Nobes
ADAM SMITH Christopher J. Berry
ADOLESCENCE Peter K. Smith
ADVERTISING Winston Fletcher
AFRICAN AMERICAN RELIGION
    Eddie S. Glaude Jr
AFRICAN HISTORY John Parker
    and Richard Rathbone
AFRICAN POLITICS Ian Taylor
AFRICAN RELIGIONS
    Jacob K. Olupona
AGEING Nancy A. Pachana
AGNOSTICISM Robin Le Poidevin
AGRICULTURE Paul Brassley and
    Richard Soffe
ALEXANDER THE GREAT
    Hugh Bowden
ALGEBRA Peter M. Higgins
AMERICAN CULTURAL HISTORY
    Eric Avila
AMERICAN HISTORY
    Paul S. Boyer
AMERICAN IMMIGRATION
    David A. Gerber
AMERICAN LEGAL HISTORY
    G. Edward White
AMERICAN POLITICAL HISTORY
    Donald Critchlow
AMERICAN POLITICAL PARTIES
    AND ELECTIONS L. Sandy Maisel
AMERICAN POLITICS
    Richard M. Valelly
THE AMERICAN PRESIDENCY
    Charles O. Jones

THE AMERICAN REVOLUTION
    Robert J. Allison
AMERICAN SLAVERY
    Heather Andrea Williams
THE AMERICAN WEST Stephen Aron
AMERICAN WOMEN'S HISTORY
    Susan Ware
ANAESTHESIA Aidan O'Donnell
ANALYTIC PHILOSOPHY
    Michael Beaney
ANARCHISM Colin Ward
ANCIENT ASSYRIA Karen Radner
ANCIENT EGYPT Ian Shaw
ANCIENT EGYPTIAN ART AND
    ARCHITECTURE Christina Riggs
ANCIENT GREECE Paul Cartledge
THE ANCIENT NEAR EAST
    Amanda H. Podany
ANCIENT PHILOSOPHY Julia Annas
ANCIENT WARFARE
    Harry Sidebottom
ANGELS David Albert Jones
ANGLICANISM Mark Chapman
THE ANGLO-SAXON AGE John Blair
ANIMAL BEHAVIOUR
    Tristram D. Wyatt
THE ANIMAL KINGDOM
    Peter Holland
ANIMAL RIGHTS David DeGrazia
THE ANTARCTIC Klaus Dodds
ANTHROPOCENE Erle C. Ellis
ANTISEMITISM Steven Beller
ANXIETY Daniel Freeman and
    Jason Freeman
APPLIED MATHEMATICS Alain Goriely

Available soon:

For more information visit our website

www.oup.com/vsi/

Adam Sharr

MODERN ARCHITECTURE

A Very Short Introduction

OXFORD
UNIVERSITY PRESS

OXFORD

UNIVERSITY PRESS

Great Clarendon Street, Oxford, OX2 6DP,
United Kingdom

Oxford University Press is a department of the University of Oxford.
It furthers the University's objective of excellence in research, scholarship,
and education by publishing worldwide. Oxford is a registered trade mark of
Oxford University Press in the UK and in certain other countries

First edition published in 2018

Impression: 1

Published in the United States of America by Oxford University Press
198 Madison Avenue, New York, NY 10016, United States of America

British Library Cataloguing in Publication Data
Data available

Library of Congress Control Number: 2018949934

ISBN 978–0–19–878344–2

Printed in Great Britain by
Ashford Colour Press Ltd, Gosport, Hampshire

To Jacob
(who, at the moment, is still very short)

Contents

Acknowledgements

For much of the 20th century, modern architecture stood for the place of the future—as related to the past—in the present. In the recent past, it's profited from some excellent historians, critics, commentators, and theorists. I'm especially grateful to five who generously read parts of the first draft of this manuscript: Nathaniel Coleman, Katie Lloyd Thomas, Juliet Odgers, Steve Parnell, and Flora Samuel. I also want to thank: Samuel Austin, Andrew Ballantyne, Tom Brigden, Martin Beattie, Kati Blom, Roger Burrows, Hugh Campbell, Prue Chiles, Hazel Cowie, Sam Clark, Kieran Connolly, James A. Craig, Martyn Dade-Robertson, Patrick Devlin, Mark Dorrian, Paul Emmons, Graham Farmer, Adrian Forty, Josep-Maria Garcia-Fuentes, Daniel Goodricke, Stephen Graham, Jonathan A. Hale, Neveen Hamza, Laura Harty, James Hegarty, Jonathan Hill, Aldric Rodriguez Iborra, Stephen Kite, Amy Kulper, David Leatherbarrow, James Longfield, Zeynep Kezer, Ashley Mason, Yasser Megahed, Mhairi McVicar, Marga Munar Bauza, Matt Ozga-Lawn, John Pendlebury, Diana Periton, Tim Pitman, Sophia Psarra, Alistair Robinson, Simon Sadler, Claire Sayner, Bernhard Schmid, Geoff Shearcroft, Mark Tewdwr-Jones, Stephen Thornton, Ray Verrall, Anthony Vidler, Geoff Vigar, Edward Wainwright, Ian Wells, Antony Wood, Richard Weston, and Ellis Woodman.

Various ideas from modern architecture remain surprisingly uncontested in present-day architectural culture, and can seem strange to an architect's clients, contractors, and fellow consultants. Through my own architectural practice, while writing this book, I've benefited from trying to rehearse some of them with: Lisa Armour-Brown and Ashley Hipkin, Iain Garfield, Ross Henderson, Steve Jackson, Stephen Pyle, Andy Ransome, Clare Rogers, Russell Smith, Tony Stevenson, and Carol Young.

I'm extremely grateful to Andrea Keegan from Oxford University Press for posing me the challenge of writing a short introduction to modern architecture, and doing it with just thirty images. Oxford's anonymous readers, and Jenny Nugee, Deborah Protheroe, Gillian Northcott Liles, and Joy Mellor made numerous indispensable contributions.

I was appointed Head of the School of Architecture, Planning and Landscape at Newcastle University, UK, part-way through writing this manuscript. Among many colleagues, Julie Sanders, Elaine Watt, Jill Mawson, and Lucy Morgan helped me to finish it.

Heartfelt thanks are due, as always, to Joanne Sayner for her tolerance, wisdom, and difficult questions. This manuscript has been in our lives only a few months fewer than our little boy. It's dedicated to Jacob, in the hope that he'll appreciate the past, and see the best of possible futures.

List of illustrations

Chapter 1
Introduction

Somewhere between 1910 and 1970, architecture changed. Now that modern architecture is familiar—and we've seen how it became both celebrated and vilified—it's hard to imagine how novel it once seemed. Expensive Western buildings became transformed from ornamented fancies, which referred to the classical and medieval pasts, into strikingly plain reflections of novel materials, technologies, and ideas. It's equally hard to remember how modern architecture promised transformation, seemingly poised to turn dirty, overcrowded cities—characterized by packed slums and Satanic mills—into spacious realms of generous housing and clean mechanized production, set in parkland. At certain times and in certain cultures, modern architecture stood for the liberation of the future from the past.

The phrase 'modern architecture' describes a spectrum of buildings and ideas. From Shakespeare's times until the 19th century, 'modern' in English meant 'up to date'. The idea of progress became important in the 19th century and that made the modern 'progressive': part of an apparently predestined course from an impoverished past, to a still inadequate present, towards an idealized future. More recently however, the term modern largely came to describe a specific time in the

20th century when many people, especially in the West, seemed persuaded that a better future was on its way.

For some historians, modern architecture refers primarily to stark white buildings from the 1920s and 1930s: crisp, hovering edifices which, so the story goes, reflected honestly their internal functions on the outside, illustrating how they were put together, highlighting the 'shock of the new'. For others, the idea of a modern architectural future had a longer history. It dated back to the Paris World's Fair of 1889, or John Ruskin's 1849 exhortations about how medieval Gothic cathedrals expressed structure honestly in stone.

Just as it's possible to argue about the beginnings of modern architecture, its demise has been much debated. For various commentators, modern architecture is over. It was supplanted by 'postmodernism' in the 1980s and 1990s, when architects became less interested in the expression of function, and returned to historical motifs (like the 1991 extension to London's National Gallery, designed by Venturi, Scott Brown and Associates), or striking shape-making of various kinds (like the sinuous Guggenheim Museum, Bilbao, 1997, designed by Frank O. Gehry's studio). For others, modern architecture—as the expression of contemporary building technologies, as the idea of making construction legible and transparent—remains current, no matter that other disciplines insist on the demise of modernity in their fields.

I'll take a long and broad view of modern architecture here, examining what Harold Rosenberg called 'the tradition of the new', arguing that it didn't just emerge fully formed in the 1910s and 1920s, or as the consequence of 19th-century pioneers, but was instead the product of two centuries of industrialization, and the global spread of industrial culture. I set out neither to promote nor condemn modern architecture. Rather, my aim is to illustrate how it was produced out of—and reflected—the cultures that constructed it. I explore it in all its strangeness and thoughtfulness, as designed by some curious, obsessive characters.

The organization of this book

Certain famous modern architects were skilled self-publicists. Memorable aphorisms, like Ludwig Mies van der Rohe's 'less is more', and Le Corbusier's 'the house is a machine for living', entered the lexicons of popular quotation. Less widely known, but chortled-at by generations of architecture students, is Louis Kahn's 1971 conversation with a brick:

> If you think of Brick, you say to Brick, 'What do you want, Brick?' And Brick says to you 'I like an Arch'. And if you say to Brick 'Look, arches are expensive and I can use a concrete lintel over you. What do you think of that Brick?' Brick says 'I like an Arch'.

This image of architect in communion with brick illustrates a point which preoccupied modern architects: that different building materials imply their own inherent logics. How particular materials go together, Kahn suggested, make certain combinations of structure, wall, and building assembly seem inevitable: brick wants to make arches; timber wants to make lattices of beams and posts; steel wants to make frames; reinforced concrete wants to make frames too, and also thin planes and big spans. You can persuade those materials to behave otherwise, but why—Kahn implied—as a thoughtful modern architect, would you do that? This was not new. In 1863, Parisian architect Eugène-Emmanuel Viollet-le-Duc wrote that any 'change of material must bring about a change of forms'. The contemporaneous German writer Gottfried Semper argued that brick, wood, and iron should be treated according to their 'statical laws'. Both responded to Ruskin's ideas about honesty to materials and the honest visual expression of the uses of a building. Their earnest morality persisted into modern architecture. And the idea that materials have their own inherent logics explains how I've organized this book.

Historians often gave architects more credit than they deserved for shaping modern architecture. Modern architects' imaginations were hugely extended by material innovations. Developments in steel and reinforced concrete radically altered possibilities for shaping buildings, as did new systems for electric lighting and handling air. These technical innovations, in turn, emerged from new cultures of industrial production. Thus, my story is organized around the technical innovations that opened up the cultural and intellectual opportunities for modern architecture to happen.

This isn't to say that architects were involved in the invention of new technologies—most weren't, and many disapproved at first—but, as Adrian Forty has argued, architects' special ability was to conjure up images for new technologies that made them seem striking and appealing. Architects didn't create steel and reinforced concrete, or fluorescent tubes and air conditioning, but they appreciated how those technologies could make the world look and feel different. And they designed knowingly in relation to imagery from other spheres, like modern art and industrial design. The British modern architect Wells Coates wrote in 1931 that there was a choice between 'the use of the new...materials as prisoners—the slaves—of old habits, old social prejudices, old *visual* prejudices; or as the means to new forms, new habits of life, a new vision'.

My story thus explores the architectural consequences of iron and steel, reinforced concrete, brick, air conditioning, and electric light to illustrate how modern architecture produced powerful cultural images expressing the potential of the future. These new technologies were not adopted by architects in a linear sequence but, to some extent, in parallel. So, each chapter here—while organized broadly in chronological order—shifts back in time to begin before the previous one ends.

Some definitions

I define modernity here as *the condition of living in an industrialized society*. Industrialized societies are those shaped by modern science and consumer technologies: by mass production, mass markets, mass consumption, mass education, and mass media; by novelty and fashion; and by accelerating globalization fuelled by the power of global finance. Underpinning industrialized societies was an idea that perpetual scientific progress operated hand in hand with economic growth, and also—sometimes—multi-party democracy. Alongside industry, work, and changing patterns of domestic life, the category of modernity encompassed ideas from art, literature, film, theatre, media, music, philosophy, and architecture: cultural endeavours reflecting modern societies, and shaping them through the reflections they offered. Modern technology, and the cultures it produced, seemed poised to liberate people from rigid constraints traditionally imposed by their gender, class, or ethnicity. But the same progress could also seem alienating—disrupting traditional communities and ways of life. Modernity thus mixed optimism about the social opportunities of technology with deep unease about its consequences. The peak of modernity occurred between the late 19th and mid-20th centuries in the West. Indeed, modernity extended beyond the West in different places at different times, sometimes associated with colonization in the 19th and 20th centuries, and sometimes with postcolonial societies.

More recently, faith in perpetual progress was shaken. Science and technology appeared fallible. Power structures linking the funding of science and political parties with industry, finance, and military endeavours became more apparent. The operation of these power structures in service of people of a particular class, ethnicity, and gender, from particular corners of the globe, was highlighted. And the vast consumption of energy and disposable goods was questioned in terms of sustainability. For these reasons, it's widely assumed that modernity—as an idea about progress—ended during the latter part of the 20th century, or at least became much more complicated. The term 'postmodern' was coined to describe what followed.

I define modern architecture here as *architecture produced out of the condition of modernity*. In particular, it's architecture that contributed to modernity, because the images of its buildings seemed to express what modernity stood for.

Modern architecture's champions referred to 'the modern movement', associating it with radical movements in art. The term also implied connections with radical political movements that its characters occasionally hooked up with, in Russia and Italy in the 1910s, and Germany and France in the 1920s. Only when tidied up by sympathetic historians in retrospect, however, did it look like a coherent movement. There were always multiple modern architectures and the term meant different things to different people at different times. In his 1896 book *Modern Architecture*, architect Otto Wagner associated the idea with the rational and honest expression of materials, structure, and function, and with the purging of unnecessary decoration—themes familiar as late as the 1970s. In the 1910s, however, quite different architectures of 'Art Nouveau', characterized by swirling floral motifs, would also have been called modern, alongside the 'expressionist' crystalline shapes of Bruno Taut's 'Crystal Chain' group. By the late 1930s, however, these counted as modern less frequently. At that time, modern architecture became more tightly defined around buildings evoking glamorous technologies of the age: cars, ocean liners, and aeroplanes. This was the so-called International Style, matching white planes with flat roofs, open plans, extensive glazing, horizontal windows, and blocks you could see below or through. By the late 1950s, multiple modern architectures proliferated again, reconsidering what then became seen as the 'early modern' architecture of the 1930s. Certain architects at that time hoped to make modern architecture more humane, dramatic, monumental, or systematically scientific. Despite these differences, the idea of a single modern movement persisted. It sounded glamorous and sold textbooks.

Modern architecture was also defined by how architects designed it. There are three primary kinds of scaled architectural drawing: the elevation, depicting a façade; the section, a vertical cut from roof to foundations showing floors stacked up; and the plan, a horizontal cut showing the layout of rooms on a floor. Where architects previously agonized over elevations, often adapting plans and sections around decisions made about the façades, modern architects prioritized the plan. They claimed that the layout of rooms—the best functional arrangement for a house, library, or office—should come first, and that elevations should be secondary. The most famous modern architect, Le Corbusier, wrote that 'the plan is the generator'. Louis Sullivan's catchy aphorism 'form ever follows function' was a slogan for this way of working. In the writings of Adolf Loos, it became elevated to a moral imperative. By the 1930s, most modern architects believed there was something truthful about designs prioritizing function, and something dishonest about designs emphasizing a building's artistic decoration. Despite the rhetoric, however, modern architects remained deeply concerned with the imagery of their buildings. Indeed, numerous modern buildings can be understood as architectural images dedicated to undermining the idea of architectural imagery.

From the 1930s, modern architecture increasingly became called 'Modernism', making it sound like a cause. The term allowed historians to characterize modern architecture as a style like other architectural styles (Neo-Classicism or Gothic Revivalism, for example). It also helped them link it to other modernisms in art and literature that similarly responded to technological cultures, industrialization, and globalization. This appealed to critics who made reputations out of classifying trends. But many modern architects thought they were isolating honest, timeless ways to design—not indulging in something as fleeting as a style—and vigorously rejected the idea.

Modernism appears with and without a capital 'm'. Some advocates of modern architecture used the capital letter to sort out buildings they felt were special symbols of the movement from buildings that were merely new. Others used it to elevate Modernism to the status of other nouns capitalized in English, like Church or God. You won't see Modern or Modernism written with a capital 'm' again here. And I'll use modernism sparingly. I don't want to make modern architecture seem more important than other architectures. Nor do I find obsessing about which famous buildings fit into which stylistic categories particularly fruitful. When studying architecture, it seems more interesting to think instead about buildings themselves: how they work, what they do, and what they say.

Having reflected on the 'modern' in 'modern architecture', it's worth pausing on 'architecture'. Nikolaus Pevsner, the prominent modern historian, famously made a distinction between architecture and building: 'A bicycle shed is a building', he wrote, 'whereas Lincoln Cathedral is a work of architecture'. Distinctions like this are widespread but obstructive. All buildings—bicycle shed or cathedral, banal office building or obsessively detailed museum—offer insights into the values of the people and cultures which produced them, illustrating the ideas informing their design, construction, and use. All are valid objects of scholarly attention. I've included (big) sheds and bridges in this book, alongside churches and high-rise towers, because they all yielded important architectural images of modernity. If anything distinguishes the buildings I've included here from others, it's that they became famous because they proved inspiring or troubling enough for people to have projected ideas about modernity onto them.

Most histories of modern architecture bring the story up to date. But, because I contend that modernity transformed into something else, my story closes in the 1970s, accepting that architecture transformed with it. This end point coincides with a time when building regulations introduced in the West made the idea of truth to materials harder to achieve at the level of architectural detail. While ideas from modern architecture remain doggedly persistent, and numerous architects still practice as paid-up modernists, ours is now the architecture of another time which will attract its own histories in due course.

Histories of the future

Modern architecture owed as much to its storytellers as its buildings. Le Corbusier's 1923 book *Towards a New Architecture*—which became admired in the Anglosphere in the 1930s—tried to establish moral and visual principles for modern architecture. Meanwhile, certain historians rewrote architectural history to make modernism its logical consequence, including Hitchcock and Johnson, whose 1932 term 'International Style' I've already mentioned, and Pevsner, whose *Pioneers of Modern Design*, 1936, sought to persuade sceptics inclined towards the past that modern architecture actually emerged from a long history. Sigfried Giedion illustrated in 1941 how architecture could be understood in terms of time and space. And in the 1960s, (Peter) Reyner Banham—'historian of the immediate future'—extended the category of architecture to include all sorts of industrial structures, technologies, and gadgets. Robert Venturi's *Complexity and Contradiction in Architecture*, 1966, reminded readers that history always infused modern architecture, and anticipated the postmodernism that followed. It's a curious quirk that modern architecture—whose most extreme forms rejected the past—was so extensively consolidated by its historians.

Architectural histories have strange conventions. Buildings are usually designed in studios full of architects and technicians, with clients, builders, engineers, and regulations that help to shape them. Nevertheless, historians mostly attribute famous buildings to a single architect—usually male, white, and Western, like most of the historians themselves—even if that individual hardly spent any time on the project. I'll use this pervasive convention here, albeit guardedly, with this reminder not to forget who it conceals. Another convention—as old as the book *The Lives of the Artists* by architect Giorgio Vasari, 1550—depicts famous architects as visionary geniuses working against the odds. This idea persists, and certain modern architects became elevated into superheroes who could do no wrong. I'll highlight one such anointed superhero in each chapter, recalling the celebrity worship that still pervades architectural culture.

Few architectural history books stray from sites of financial and cultural power. Most discuss buildings that were novel when they were constructed becoming models for others that followed, built in places with the wealth necessary to make them, the cultural sensibilities that prized their novelty, and celebrated by local critics influential enough to get them widely noticed. Architectural historians now worry about this, about repeatedly retelling dominant but partisan stories. To compensate, they've worked to make their histories more diverse and inclusive, to illustrate who has the power to build what, when, where, how, and for whom. A very short book like this inevitably has to omit far more than it includes, so I've focused here on a small selection of buildings that also account for bigger cultural ideas. I emphasize *what* modern architecture was like, *why* it was like that, and *how* it was imagined, more than the global patterns of *where* and *when*. This approach helps me to argue that buildings themselves should be the primary source of architectural research: that every building—cathedral or bicycle shed, glamorous gallery or your own home—contains architectural, cultural, technical, and historical knowledge. It also emphasizes the buildings that you need to know to talk knowledgably with others who think they already know about modern architecture. Its consequence, however, is to reinforce the Euro-American mainstream, omitting buildings and characters from other contexts. I've tried to mitigate this by including some less familiar projects and introducing some familiar examples in less familiar ways. Ultimately though, I hope this book will encourage you to read further, to go beyond buildings designed largely by white Western men in the most powerful countries in the world to explore less-charted but equally important modern architectures.

Chapter 2
Iron and steel

A bridge to modernity

My story about modern architecture begins with an iron bridge completed in 1779 (Figure 1). It's only questionably modern and, for that matter, only questionably architecture. But it illustrates the industrial cultures where modern architecture started to form.

The bridge was made from five arched cast-iron ribs, spreading their load to two masonry abutments, assembled without using nuts and bolts. The bridge became so famous, because its construction was so novel, that the town forming around it took its name. Ironbridge, sat in a mineral-rich gorge in England's West Midlands, became the crucible of the 18th century's Industrial Revolution.

The Iron Bridge was proposed by an architect, Thomas Pritchard—and it bears his ornamental flourishes—but it was executed under the direction of a fabricator, Abraham Darby III. The Darby family's Coalbrookdale foundry was then a world leader in iron production. The first Abraham Darby had worked out how to use coked coal, rather than charcoal made from timber, to raise temperatures in the blast furnaces where iron was made. This yielded consistently higher quality iron at lower cost, made in

1. Iron Bridge, Ironbridge, Shropshire, UK, completed 1779.
A technological wonder of its time, which displayed and promoted a set of emerging ideas about what later became called modernity. While built from a new material—iron—it still subscribed to the traditional image of a bridge built in masonry. (Fabricator: Abraham Darby III; Architect: Thomas Pritchard.)

large furnaces that could run continuously. Coalbrookdale's innovations in the volume production of iron, and growing experience in fabricating iron components, contributed not just to the bridge but to the whole Industrial Revolution.

The Iron Bridge introduces four themes that recur throughout this book. First, it indicates the beginnings of a shift in global culture, over two centuries, from artisan manufacturing towards mass production. While the components of the bridge were sourced nearby—using local ironstone, clay, sand, limestone, coal, and water—it was assembled from a limited number of repeated components. This anticipated a huge cultural shift. New technologies enabled cheaper and quicker manufacturing, opening up industrial production in fields—like textiles and furniture—that were previously the province of artisans. This new industrial culture usually separated design from making. Where seamstresses or joiners, for example, made design decisions with their tools in hand, based on their experience of working materials, designers began to emerge in various fields who imagined artefacts and drew them for others to make. In consequence, makers' skills became increasingly channelled into the accurate reproduction of given designs. While the figure of the architect emerged well before mass production—out of ancient origins rediscovered in the 15th century—the modern idea of the professional who draws buildings got shaped in association with this emerging idea of design. The modern notion of construction as an industry emerged with it, gradually replacing old priorities of art and craft in building with new ideas about efficiency and predictability.

Second, the Iron Bridge illustrates the emergence of the idea of a single global culture. Early mass production, like that in the Severn gorge, quickly exceeded the stock of local raw materials. The hunger of new factories, from blast foundries to textile mills, and the hunger of their owners for profit, meant that materials and workers were sought elsewhere as local supplies dwindled. Associated ideas about raw materials being commodities, and individual workers combining into a collective called labour, started to form the modern habit of imagining the world in terms of resources to be exploited.

The more the machines produced, and the greater the demand for their cheaper products, the wider the distribution of those products. Transport infrastructures were constructed to bring in material and labour resources, and to ship out manufactured ones. For example, in a short time at the end of the 18th century, the River Severn flowing through Ironbridge became linked to other rivers via a canal network connecting British cities, joined with ports linked to global shipping. By the middle of the 19th century, these canals were supplanted by railways that could move more goods and people at higher speeds. In the later 20th century, railways themselves became overtaken by motorways, air transport, and containerization. Thus, the transport infrastructures made necessary by industry expanded and accelerated during the modern period. They produced in their wake a global culture where industry flourished, and where global consumption and mass travel seemed to shrink distances and cultural differences.

This alliance of trade, industry, and shipping fuelled Western countries' colonization of parts of Africa, Asia, and the Americas during the 18th and 19th centuries. For example, in northeast England, on the River Tyne rather than the Severn, Lord Armstrong's Elswick Works produced munitions, ships, and hydraulic construction equipment. These were sold without scruple to armies, militia, governments, and corporations including—famously—both sides of the same conflict. Fuelled by technocratic enterprises like Armstrong's, colonialism opened up what became imagined as the material and human resources of conquered lands to the new industries. It brought enormous wealth to European and North American captains of industry, and often significant suffering to the places and peoples plundered. The novel goods and values exported by new industries celebrated global commerce, market forces, and the idea of industry as progress—which then seemed to become their inevitable consequence.

Just as the idea of a single global culture is latent in the reproduced components of the Iron Bridge, so too are modern ideas of economy and technology. Taken together, these constitute the third theme I argue that the bridge illustrates. New industries—like Coalbrookdale Foundry—produced massive social and cultural change in the 18th and early 19th centuries. The population of England's West Midlands, like much of Western Europe and later the USA, shifted largely from rural agricultural work to urban industrial work. Growing urban populations sustained industrial production and encouraged the consumption of its outputs. The massive changes that successive generations observed—the emergence of labour-saving devices, for example, from the mangle to the fridge; or wonder drugs from anaesthetics to antibiotics—became inextricably linked in people's minds with the idea of technology. And this association of technology with progress, popularized through novel innovations, became inseparable from modernity.

The reach of manufacturing industries and transport infrastructures increasingly extended into almost every facet of everyday life. And the global economy on which the modern idea of progress relied became increasingly pervasive. The word 'economy' once referred to the frugal management of a household, to an ancient villa and its land, sustaining a society of people living and working there, standing for the idea that just enough was sufficient. But the substantial costs of industrial production, and the extravagant profits to be made from it, made loan finance—once condemned as the evil of 'usury'—more culturally acceptable. The financiers made the biggest profits of all. In the late 19th and early 20th centuries, colonialism and transport globalized finance at least as much as they globalized the new industries.

The Iron Bridge also introduces a fourth idea, about architectural 'imageability'. Whether or not it was the first iron bridge in the world—that's been debated—it was the first whose image became widely distributed. At the time, its spindly see-through structure looked remarkable to eyes accustomed to brick or stone. How could something so apparently fragile be evidently so strong? The structure drew artists intrigued to depict it. An exhibition celebrating the bridge's bicentenary in 1979, held at London's Royal Academy, collected over fifty images made between 1750 and 1830. Pictures of the bridge, sat in its picturesque gorge, symbolized the wonder of technology. And new media technologies—like engraving and printing—allowed the widespread distribution of its imagery, lending it global significance. Like many famous works of modern architecture, images of the Iron Bridge seemed to surpass the structure's own physical presence. Its depiction, in paintings and engravings, acquired a currency beyond the original, admired by a much bigger audience than had seen the bridge first hand, making it a striking symbol of the idea of the new.

The Iron Bridge also illustrates imageability in another way. Made in iron, assembled from multiple components, it's constructed in the same form as a masonry arch. Effectively, it took what was then the known image of a bridge—the arch—and reproduced it in a new material. Arches suit how brick and stone behave in compression (when loaded with weight from above), distributing loads evenly from central keystones to the ground. Iron, meanwhile, has different properties. Made into chain links and cables, it performs better in tension (where forces tend to pull it apart). This was exploited in 1801 in the inventor James Finlay's design for Jacob's Creek Bridge in Westmorland County, Pennsylvania, suspending a deck from iron trusses and establishing the basic components of the modern suspension bridge. Later structures, like engineer Thomas Telford's Menai Bridge in North Wales, 1820, and Isambard Kingdom Brunel's Clifton Suspension Bridge in Bristol, UK, 1834, consolidated a new logic for iron construction and a new image for iron bridges derived more directly from the logic of the material. While Ironbridge's Iron Bridge was innovative, it was nevertheless constrained in its designers' imaginations by their prevailing idea of what a bridge ought to look like.

This raises an important point—that there remain deeply embedded cultural assumptions about the imagery of certain types of buildings and structures. Children learn culturally coded images so they can distinguish a living room from a street, for example, or a house from an office, and people think they know what buildings look like after that. But these codes become so powerful that designers take time to challenge them. More significantly, they become so powerful that people find it hard to accept new architectural images when familiar ones are challenged.

I want to mention one last way that the Iron Bridge anticipated modern architecture. Recent surveys of the bridge showed how its repeated components were adjusted individually, during manufacturing, to fit their neighbours. There is, it's been shown, tens of millimetres' difference between seemingly identical components. The ideal of mass production in architecture has always been that: an ideal. Despite ongoing enthusiasm for industrialization, particular builders usually constructed modern buildings on particular sites for particular clients, from the drawings of particular designers. During the 20th century, it grew less common for architects to design every detail of buildings and more common for them to specify mass-produced components, like prefabricated doorsets, roof trusses, or kitchen units. Only rarely, however, were whole buildings mass produced. Nevertheless, the image of mass production remained insistent in modern architecture, to the point where bespoke buildings were sometimes made to look prefabricated to assert their modernity. Commentators keen on industrial production argued repeatedly over more than a century that prefabrication was the imminent future of architecture, without it being fulfilled on any scale.

Iron and modern science

It's remarkable that iron manufacturing ever became widespread. Iron is extracted from mineral, from iron ore, at a boiling point of 1,535 °C, involving fierce heat and light. This doesn't produce pure iron but an impure substance—named 'pig iron' after the shape of the casting beds once used—which is hard and brittle. This then gets remelted, during which time it is carefully 'decarburized' to control the level of carbon and impurities like sulphur, improving the strength of the material, before being left once again to cool.

It's sometimes claimed that the engineering innovations of the Industrial Revolution emerged from modern science. But, until the mid-19th century, the history of iron manufacturing was largely the history of trial and error. Telford's and Brunel's bridges, for example, were worked out from instinct and experience, preceding any comprehensive theory of structures. Thomas Newcomen's and James Watt's 18th-century work developing steam engines—despite the latter's theoretical research into chemistry late in life—emerged from the workshop and not from calculation. Likewise, the Darby family's endeavours at Coalbrookdale were based on testing and observation. Early 19th-century engineering aspired to scientific authority, however, and science encouraged the culture in which engineering flourished.

The modern idea of science—seeking mathematical descriptions of natural phenomena out of systematic experiments—emerged in the West in the 16th and 17th centuries. It was popularized by the reputations of figures like Nicolaus Copernicus (1473–1543), who proposed in 1549 that the Earth revolved around the sun and not vice versa, and Isaac Newton (1642–1727), whose physics linked astronomical observations with Earth-bound ones, producing theories of optics and calculus. Theories like these emphasized rational analysis, encouraging a gradual shift from a God-fearing medieval society, where humans imagined themselves subservient to the natural world, towards a 20th-century secular condition where science and technology made humans feel they could control the world.

After the construction of the Iron Bridge, there were rapid improvements in making iron stronger and more predictable. Henry Cort patented the puddling process in 1783, stirring molten iron to draw in oxygen and burn out carbon. In 1832,

John Gibbons tried different geometries of blast furnace, significantly increasing production capacity. By the mid-19th century, wrought iron became a reliable construction material, albeit that mass-produced components were still tested by hand and eye to ensure their soundness. It was only towards the end of that century that the design of iron structures became more scientific, when engineers learnt to calculate stresses and deflections accurately.

The St Geneviève Library in Paris was designed by architect Henri Labrouste between 1838 and 1850, at the point between early experiments in mass producing iron components and their widespread use in building, between trial and error and applied science. The twin iron vaults of its lofty reading room were tied to thick stone piers lining the perimeter, connected by arched openings containing tall bookstacks with windows above (Figure 2).

2. St Geneviève Library, Paris, France, 1850. Slender iron vaults contained by masonry walls, built at a time poised between trial and error in engineering and the emergence of reliable structural calculations. Its architect, Henri Labrouste, sought a new resolution between novel technologies of construction and the idea that architecture could be a vital expression of culture.

In conjunction with the building's spare decoration, the vaults anticipated the light and airy qualities of modern buildings.

St Geneviève Library was controversial in mid-19th-century Paris. It rejected the prevailing idea, promoted by that city's famous architecture school, L'École des Beaux-Arts, that architecture should involve the artful composition of decorative forms derived from scholarly study of the orders of classical architecture. The library instead appeared strikingly plain. Structure and decoration were effectively separated out. Decoration was applied to panels set into, and between, the primary structure, expressing the structural design of the building visually. These ideas chimed with emerging architectural thinkers, notably John Ruskin, whose book *Modern Painters* (first published anonymously in 1843) argued that art should be honest to the realities of nature; expanded in his *Seven Lamps of Architecture*, 1849, which promoted truth—including the honest expression of structural forces—as essential to beauty and life. For these reasons—of material, structure, and decoration—the St Geneviève library was later claimed as a progenitor of modern architecture. But it also stood for emerging modernity in another way.

Labrouste knew the novelist Victor Hugo, who remains famous for *The Hunchback of Notre Dame*, written at the time of the July Revolution in France in 1830 and published in 1831. Hugo asked Labrouste to comment on a draft chapter criticizing scholarly Beaux Arts architecture. Set in Notre Dame Cathedral in 1482, the chapter follows an encounter between archdeacon Claude Frollo and a character who turns out to be King Louis XI. At a key moment, Frollo glances down at a printed book on the table and then up through a window to the towers of the Cathedral. 'This' (the book), he reflects wistfully, 'will kill that' (the Cathedral). Hugo's novel was set when the invention of the printing press, by Johannes Gutenberg in 1436, allowed the widespread distribution of books. But Hugo made a contemporary point. He claimed, via Frollo, that architecture was understood before printing, before mass production, not just in terms of shelter or as a container of human activities but instead as a form of knowledge. And that knowledge—carved in stone in the great buildings of human culture—was a kind of cultural currency that could be read by the people whose lives those great buildings touched. Architecture, he suggested, was a force for social integration because it expressed shared symbols. Hugo's character argued that architecture was losing its uniting power to the page, prophesizing that the spread of Copernican and Newtonian science, through printing, would encourage the culture of industrialization to take over every facet of human life. Hugo thus took aim at the Beaux Arts architects who derived their designs from book learning, copying, and recopying forms from the Greeks and Romans, forgetting, he thought, how to think for themselves. They made empty copies of ancient architecture, he implied, in a city where Notre Dame showed how architecture once embodied the latest knowledge, and where it could do that again.

The historian Neil Levine argued that Labrouste's design for his strange, plain library—with its spindly iron vaults and resistance to Classical style—was an optimistic response to Hugo's criticism: an attempt to make architecture a cultural force again, this time reflecting the 19th century's emerging knowledge. The library's plain stone façades were carved with 810 names in twenty-seven panels, presenting a roll call of thinkers collected in the library (all male), organized in chronological order from the Old Testament figure Moses to the Swedish scientist Bezelius, who died in 1848 when the names were carved. The architecture of the library thus echoed and celebrated the printed page. If the book had killed ancient architecture, as Hugo supposed, then St Geneviève Library suggested that architecture could be made afresh out of the new scientific world of the book. The names on the library's façades described the huge intellectual shift from medieval European cultures dominated by a single Christian God, to the so-called rational thought of 19th-century modern science and technology. Designed at the beginning of the so-called Second Republic in France, the names also described a parallel, connected shift towards ideas of modern industrial democracy, away from the absolute monarchies of the European past. The library's vaults—made in iron, the technological material of the moment—were physically and metaphorically tied to stone walls whose carved names expressed the intellectual forces that iron seemed to represent. The vaults stood for their architect's premonition that a meaningful modern architecture was possible, derived from modern science and the technical culture of industrial production.

The library highlighted an apparent tension emerging at that time between engineering and architecture, between new technologies of construction and an older idea of architecture as an expression of culture. How, it seemed to ask, might the organization and imagery of architecture embrace the culture of modernity? This fraught question preoccupied certain architects well into the next century.

Space and industrial culture

Railways arrived in European and American cities in the mid-19th century, and their promoters' lofty terminus stations—frequently boasting dramatic iron vaults—became understood in retrospect as further addressing this question, shifting attention from architecture's façades to its interior spaces. St Pancras Station, London, 1868, is a famous example. Its train shed's arched trusses—designed by engineer William Barlow—soared 75 metres over the tracks without intermediate columns. Still influenced by older ideas about civic decorum, however, this striking display of iron's potential was enclosed within masonry walls and concealed from the street by the ten-storey Midland Grand Hotel: a Gothic Revival fairy tale decorated with gables and fancy balconies, designed by architect George Gilbert Scott. Architecture and engineering, trainshed and station building, were frequently separated—physically and intellectually—in such railway terminals. But it was the iron sheds that most captured peoples' imaginations. It's no coincidence that painter Édouard Manet chose the trainshed of a Parisian station, buzzing with activity and filled evocatively with steam, to depict the emerging atmosphere of modernity—rather than the conventional station building—in his painting *Gare Saint-Lazare*, 1873.

At that time, engineers—not architects—were most comfortable with the structural opportunities, imagery, and space-enclosing potential of iron. Some, like Gustave Eiffel and Joseph Paxton, came from working-class backgrounds and transcended rigid class structures through entrepreneurship and technical cunning. Paxton and Eiffel cultivated the image of self-made practical people that just got on with things, in opposition to scholarly gentleman architects who, the implication was, dithered and delayed. They reimagined iron not just as a material for roofs within masonry walls, but as structural framing that could define the spaces of buildings. Indeed, they helped define the idea of 'space' as the end result of modern architecture: a notion still forming as recently as the 1920s.

Paxton was a gardener turned engineer. He earned his reputation as the Duke of Devonshire's fixer, transforming the Duke's park at Chatsworth, UK, with hydraulic fountains, water displays, and a new village to replace one previously disrupting the Duke's view. Paxton's iron-framed glass house there—the Great Conservatory, 1837—inspired the commission for another at London's Kew Gardens, 1849, housing a giant waterlily 'found' in the colony of British Guiana. When a pet project of Queen Victoria's consort, Prince Albert—for a temporary Great Exhibition of technological wonders and colonial 'curiosities' in London's Hyde Park—ran into difficulties in 1851, Paxton proposed a giant greenhouse to contain the exhibits: a 'Crystal Palace' made from mass-produced components—conceived for speed and efficiency of construction (Figure 3).

3. Crystal Palace, London, UK, 1851. A temporary display-case for globalized modernity, constructed with great ingenuity in iron and glass. It illustrated vividly the emerging connections between global finance and colonial exploitation, between ideas about progress and a universal free market, and industrial production and the idea of the state.

Paxton devised a system of structural iron elements holding the largest sheets of glass then available, fixed into timber 'Paxton gutters' supported on a grid of iron trusses, columns, and beams. Those trusses were raised into place using horse power, aided by counter-weighted blocks. Special wagons were designed, whose wheels fitted into the gutters, on which glaziers lay to fix the panes quickly. Bolt holes in the ironwork were machined in the foundry to save filing them smooth on site. And special machines were designed to produce several grooved and bevelled sash-bars at once out of a single plank of timber. The shell of the Crystal Palace—then the largest enclosed space in the world—was erected in just four months. Opening panels were added at high level to extract rising hot air, and a timber slatted floor allowed cool air to be drawn in to replace it at low level, with the Paxton gutters profiled to collect condensation. These climate control measures were carefully considered but they couldn't mitigate the overheating and overlighting problems of putting an exhibition in a large greenhouse in summer, and various exhibitors—including Armstrong's Elswick Works and Coalbrookdale Foundry—hung giant drapes to shade their exhibits. Attracting visitors in vast numbers, the exhibition illustrated modern ideas and helped establish a new popular enchantment with technological progress. The Crystal Palace stood for fresh mythologies celebrating rational science and technical innovation, and a gradual shift away from traditional religious mythologies. Moreover, it served as a display case for the emerging products of modern globalized trade, illustrating vividly the burgeoning connections between global finance and colonial exploitation, ideas about progress and a universal free market, and industrial production and the idea of the state.

Refining ideas about mass production already latent in the Iron Bridge, the Crystal Palace also anticipated the modern idea of space. Visitors circulated inside its grid of slender columns and spidery trusses, with countless glimpses appearing and disappearing in a perpetual interlacing of structure. In long perspective, the grids of columns and glazing bars stretched almost to infinity. The palace's volume thus exemplified the mathematical conception of space: as a grid measured in equal increments on x, y, and z axes, as a field extending to infinity in all directions.

If moving around the Crystal Palace felt strikingly new, then the first experiences of climbing the curving latticework of Eiffel's Tower must have seemed something else again. Gustave Eiffel, son of a German forester, began as an apprentice engineer before founding a design-build firm serving the railway boom, opening metal workshops in a Parisian suburb. He made a reputation building large-span iron bridges: at Oporto, Portugal, 1875; and the world's largest arch, plus a series of pylons, at Garabit in France's Massif Central, 1884. Eiffel also engineered the

Statue of Liberty—shipped to New York as a gift from France, 1881—developing a mathematical solution for the tricky structural problem of raising Liberty's torch-bearing arm outwards from her body.

Eiffel's tower was the centrepiece of another temporary exhibition of technological wonders—the 1889 Paris World's Fair—housed in pavilions around its base. Designed for rapid construction, it tapped his previous experience. The tower was effectively a giant bridge pylon without the bridge, sat on foundations made using pressurized waterproof caissons, invented for building footings in rivers, allowing it to be constructed on sodden ground.

Opened at a time when few aviators had flown, and aerial views were figments of artists' imaginations, the public found the tower's three lofty viewing platforms spectacular. Equally striking was the experience of moving upwards through its structural legs in innovative elevators, themselves at the forefront of technology. Glimpses soared skyward, framing distant prospects: a cinematic experience before the popularization of cinema. Spiral stairs—sometimes locked deep in the structure and sometimes flying precariously outside—became panoramic viewing devices. The tower was not universally popular, especially among Paris's elite—one of whom quipped that he preferred to eat at its restaurants because it was only there that he couldn't see it on the skyline. Sensitive to such criticism, Eiffel talked up the tower's patriotic role for making military observations in the event of invasion, and topped it with a meteorological laboratory to associate the tower with scientific enterprise. And it quickly became a tourist staple, now characterizing Paris in countless depictions, models, and novelty paperweights.

Around the time the Eiffel Tower was imagined, the idea of space was being contested in German language art criticism by theorists like Conrad Fiedler, Gottfried Semper, and August Schmarsow. In 1846, Karl Bötticher had understood architectural style as an integration of systems of production and symbolization, proposing a new, similar, integration for iron. In 1878, Semper argued that architecture should express, monumentally, the structures of society. Architecture, he believed, should give order to culture, and symbolize culture, particularly through its *Bekleidung*, meaning 'clothing' or 'cladding'. That word 'cladding' became important. It helped modern architects to imagine façades as curtains hung around spaces, rather than as heavy structures enclosing them. Meanwhile, Schmarsow's 'room theory', 1893, argued that dynamic bodily movement around space offered a better way to appreciate architecture than the static viewing of forms.

Adrian Forty has highlighted that such theories about space—which entered English-language debates about modern architecture only in the 20th century via writers including Adolf Loos, Alois Riegel, and Siegfried Giedion—were adopted only imprecisely by modern architects, who conflated them awkwardly. Forty reflected how modern architects came to understand space—imprecisely—as both something static, contained within walls, and something dynamic, flowing through architecture. They imagined it as an abstract mathematical grid but also understood it from the bodily viewpoint of individuals moving around. They saw space as simultaneously tightly bounded, and with infinite extent. And they imagined it both as an abstract idea, and as 'stuff' that architects could shape. The emerging vocabulary of space in modern architecture was thus sometimes muddled. But it's no coincidence that it began forming when the fleshless skeletons of the early railway terminals, Crystal Palace, and Eiffel Tower were constructed, because the heightened experiences of those structures illustrated vividly how the idea of space could be imagined.

Sullivan, Wright, and the separation of wall from structure

A sequence of innovations in the latter part of the 19th century transformed iron technology, resulting in the widespread production of a less brittle variant called mild steel. The inventor Henry Bessemer successfully blew cold air through molten iron at his London bronze-powder factory in 1856, wholly 'decarburising' it. He licensed his process to manufacturers, but it turned out that his innovation relied on low-phosphorous iron ore—which wasn't widely available—and it stalled. It took amateur chemist Sidney Gilchrist Thomas to resolve how to remove phosphorous from iron to solve the problem, successfully producing a batch of steel in April 1879. Parallel, developments in iron rolling—by John Alleyne, for example, to fabricate sections of St Pancras station's roof—matured through the 1860s. By 1890, the combination of the basic Bessemer process with improved rolling mills—alongside other refinements—resulted in bigger sections and longer lengths of steel whose chemistry could be controlled to achieve different material properties. In architecture, this meant that trusses and arches made of smaller, brittle iron components could be replaced, up to certain lengths, by single, ductile steel beams or columns. And trusses made of mild steel elements could cover longer spans. Steel construction thus became easier, faster, and cheaper than iron. The new material eventually yielded new architectural imagery, but it took architects decades to work that out.

By 1890, technical initiative in steel production had shifted from Europe to America. Chicago was an important centre; characterized, into the 20th century, by sparks from its Bessemer converters puncturing night-time views of Lake Michigan. Various architects from Chicago's substantial German immigrant community knew Semper's ideas, but the rapid development of steel-framed buildings there owed more to commercial motivations than theoretical ones. Chicago was destroyed in a catastrophic fire in 1871. As reconstruction gathered pace, soaring land values encouraged developers and architects to build high, maximizing the lettable area on each plot to maximize revenues. After the inventor Elisha Otis made hydraulic elevators safe, increasing the number of floors that could be accessed easily, the primary constraint on tall buildings became the capacity for structural masonry to bear load. The eighteen-storey Monadnock Building in Chicago's downtown 'Loop', 1893, designed by Burnham and Root, demonstrated the limits of what was possible in brick, its massive flared plinth illustrating the bulk of masonry needed to support the walls above.

The idea that steel frames could exceed the height limits of brickwork came not from architects but the local steel industry. The first building to hang its external walls from a Bessemer steel frame was the Home Insurance Building in the Loop, designed by William LeBaron Jenney, 1885; followed by Holabird and Roche's Tacoma Building, 1888. Rapid construction was achieved by suspending brick, stone, and terracotta work from the frame, permitting its completion in advance of the external walls. Those walls—no longer loadbearing—thus became separated conceptually from the building's structure, echoing Semper's ideas about cladding. Louis Sullivan, of Chicago firm Adler and Sullivan, developed this approach in the Wainwright Building, St Louis, 1890, and the Guaranty Building, Buffalo, 1895. However, just as Ironbridge's iron bridge took the shape of a masonry arch, early steel-framed buildings designed by Chicago architects seemed constrained by established architectural imagery. Sullivan initially understood these projects primarily as a decorative problem about the proper expression of tall buildings, more than an opportunity for a new architectural logic.

Adler and Sullivan's substantial, complex, intricately detailed Auditorium Building in Chicago's Loop was completed in 1889, wrapping an opera house with offices, hotel rooms, and a seventeen-storey tower. Its ingenious section, constructed in steel frame within masonry walls, resolved practically the differing needs of diverse accommodation. The theatre was the first lit by electric light, also employing a novel system to circulate air. And its innovative steel and concrete 'raft' foundations were loaded up with weights that were removed while the building was constructed to avoid different parts settling at different rates. Integrating its framed structure with new building services, the Auditorium Building seemed to be imagined as a technological machine.

Critic Colin Rowe argued in a 1956 essay, 'Chicago Frame', that—although Sullivan and his contemporaries didn't grasp the full implications of what they were doing—they changed architecture. They integrated new technologies into building, valuing practicality, simplicity, and innovation. More importantly, they pointed the way towards a new steel-framed architectural logic, illustrating the separation of cladding from structure. Rowe emphasized the significance of this. 'The frame has come to possess a value for contemporary architecture,' he wrote,

> equivalent to that of the column for classical antiquity and the Renaissance...The frame establishes throughout the building a common ratio to which all the parts are related; and, like the vaulting bay in the Gothic cathedral, it prescribes a system to which all parts are subordinate.

Rowe linked the innovations of downtown Chicago's steel-framed 'skyscrapers' with the work of another architect working in that city's suburbs, Frank Lloyd Wright. Wright, who assisted Adler and Sullivan with the Auditorium Building, tested a set of ideas through a sequence of brick- and timber-built houses. These included: the Ward Willits House, Highland Park, Illinois, 1901; Darwin Martin House, Buffalo, 1904; and Frederick Robie House, Chicago, 1907. Before modernity, most buildings in the West were constructed from masonry and timber: a combination controlled by the timber sizes that could be cut efficiently from logs, preferring floor spans of 6 metres or less. Masonry and timber thus tend to produce groups of rectangular rooms enclosed by loadbearing walls holding up the floors, their architectural logic implying a series of cellular rooms surrounded by heavy walls with small openings. Wright's designs tested, within the constraints of those materials, how far conventional four-square masonry boxes could be dissolved. He experimented with: interlocking spaces at the corners of rooms, achieved using concealed steel lintels; a central hearth expressed as a 'pinwheel' around which those interlocking spaces were arranged; horizontal lines expressed in roofs and window strips to cheat the appearance of weighty masonry; and interior spaces linked to their surrounding landscape by loggias and plane walls extending outwards from the buildings.

Images of Wright's work were published in Germany in 1911. They became influential in Europe, like images of Chicago's steel-framed towers had previously, and both contributed to the slow emergence of a distinctive architectural expression for the steel frame there during the first half of the 20th century. While the frame developed quickly as a commercial and technical expedience in America, straightforwardly symbolizing trade and industry, Rowe argued, European architects only embraced it slowly, agonizing about it instead as a new spatial idea.

New images of modernity

The architectural idea of the steel frame became represented strikingly in Vladimir Tatlin's Monument to the Third International, 1920—an unbuilt project for which only a handful of drawings and model photographs survive. The Monument followed the 1917 Russian Revolution, when communists deposed the ruling elite, and began instituting new patterns of collective living. It was claimed for 'constructivism': a movement calling for art to 'go into the factory, where the real body of life is made', rejecting elite art to propose instead 'non-utilitarian constructions', fusing life with art through industry and mass production. Far from the rectangular grids of office buildings in Chicago, Tatlin's tower proposed a leaning spiral of columns and diagonal bracing, propped on an inclined pylon, with three glass rooms locked within. A cube, housing legislative assemblies, would revolve on its axis once a year. Above that, a pyramid for executive bodies would revolve once a month. On top of that, a cylinder, rotating once a day, would issue forth newspapers, proclamations, and pamphlets (spinning the spin doctors!). The tower's form derived from structural logic but was conceived primarily as an image of dynamism, symbolizing agitation and propaganda: a twisting motion frozen in steel, with mobile rooms inside. It reinvented Pieter Bruegel the Elder's famous 1563 painting of the Tower of Babel, and the Eiffel Tower, substituting their supposedly static images with a dynamic depiction of space. And space, here, was not layered into rectilinear floors and rooms but instead became a remarkable three-dimensional volume. The image of Tatlin's tower was unique in modern architecture, sticking in architects' imaginations.

Another image of the steel frame that became a key reference was the administration block of the Fagus shoe-last factory at Afeld, Germany, 1913, designed by Walter Gropius and Hannes Meyer (Figure 4). It's the first project I've discussed here that no-one would dispute calling modern—sometimes presented as a decisive step in liberating construction from artistic ornament. While Gropius's star has waned in histories of modern architecture, he was equal in fame to Le Corbusier in the 1930s and 1940s. The Fagus factory was striking for three novel elements. First, in front of its steel columns faced in brick were large panels of glass, hung from the frame, seemingly applied to the walls as planes. This was subsequently hailed (inaccurately) as the first glass 'curtain wall'—named after Semper's ideas. Second, the traditional pitched roof was rejected, in favour of a flat roof (in fact laid with a slight 'fall' for draining rainwater), an element that became an inescapable image of modernity. Third, structural steel columns were shifted away from the corners of the building where, instead, the glass curtains met at a slender steel glazing bar, with opening lights provided right at the junction. At a time when masonry walls were normal, always thickest at corners for structural reasons, this detail—linked to Wright's opening up

4. Administration block for the Fagus factory, Afeld, Germany, 1913. A key reference for early modern architects. Its distinctive components—flat roof, structural frame, 'curtain walls', and corner windows—became decisive elements of what Reyner Banham later called modern architecture's 'teenage uniform'. (Architects: Walter Gropius and Hannes Meyer.)

of corners—appeared strikingly light and free-floating, apparently suggesting that interior and exterior spaces could flow into one another. Thus, the corner window—liberated from structural constraints by technology—became another key element of modern architecture.

Inspired by Wright's houses, architects continued to test how spaces could be imagined if rigid masonry rooms became dissolved and walls became understood instead as surfaces in space. Steel allowed floors to be supported on columns or walls in fewer places than timber. Rather than enclosing a series of cells, walls could thus be reimagined as screening but not enclosing activities, separating them but not parcelling them up into compartments: as free-standing planes within larger spaces.

These planes could be imagined as slipping out of buildings, past a perimeter glass screen, blurring divisions between inside and outside, encouraged by the notion of 'space' as flowing and fluid.

This idea was influenced by modern painting in the late 1910s and early 1920s. Cubist paintings, like those of Fernand Léger and Juan Gris—or Expressionist paintings like Wassily Kandinsky's—broke up and abstracted figures and everyday objects into fragmented compositions using flattened perspectives and multiple perspective viewpoints. Rather than depicting conventional scenes, these painters instead composed lines and blocks of colour in the space of the painting. Various modern architects imagined they were doing something similar, arranging walls as lines and planes in space, and only then making a weathertight enclosure around them. And their plan drawings sometimes looked like compositions by Kandinsky or Léger.

A house in Utrecht, the Netherlands, planned for a young widow, Truus Schröder-Schräder, and her three children, by furniture designer Gerrit Rietveld, 1924, provided an extraordinary demonstration of this architecture of planes (Figure 5). Client and designer egged each other on to make something remarkable, and the small house seemed less like a building than a giant piece of inhabitable furniture. Certain walls were imagined as sliding or folding planes. Key furniture elements were fitted, with mobile pieces expressed as folding and sliding planes at another scale. Most of the detached furniture was also mobile. Rooms could be opened up in the daytime while, in the evening, walls could be slid out to enclose a bedroom and bathroom with, for example, a sofa folding into a bed and a table hinged down. Incorporating the latest technology—mains electricity, central heating, and even an early dishwasher—the Schröder House was delightfully gadgety.

Constructionally, it was a hybrid of steel, masonry, and reinforced concrete, composed to achieve artistic effects. But it was

5. Schröder House, Utrecht, the Netherlands, 1924. Walls, balconies, and columns oversail one another to suggest a collection of free-standing planes grouped artistically in space. Primary colours were artfully applied to the edges of surfaces, inside and out, to heighten the visual illusion of floating surfaces. Constructionally, it is a hybrid of steel, masonry, and reinforced concrete combined to achieve artistic effects. (Designer: Gerrit Rietveld.)

immediately striking. Its elevations were imagined not as independent faces, but as parts of a three-dimensional composition of interior and exterior planes, articulated by hingeing, folding, and sliding elements. Slender steel columns appeared to suspend planes in mid-air. Walls, balconies, and supports over-sailed one another to suggest, visually, a collection of free-standing objects grouped artistically in space, clearly different from loadbearing masonry walls. Primary colours—red, yellow, and blue—were artfully applied to the edges of surfaces, inside and out, against a backdrop of white, to heighten the visual illusion of floating surfaces. These colours related to cubist and expressionist art, specifically the contemporary Dutch art movement De Stijl (The Style). The result was a striking demonstration of a planar architectural logic whose potential was extended by modern materials.

Gropius developed his articulation of the Fagus Factory, without its brick panels, at another framed structure finished in 1926: the headquarters of the Bauhaus school of design in Dessau, Germany, where he became the first head. The building consolidated an appreciation of the visual detachment of planes, as developed through the work of Wright, De Stijl, and Rietveld. 'Part hippie commune, part zen monastery' (as Richard Weston put it), the curriculum of Gropius's Bauhaus reflected its new home—emphasizing engineering, geometry, and industrial craft, with the addition of radical politics. In its early years, it was imagined as a reinvented medieval craft guild, and Bauhaus students worked directly with materials, including steel. They integrated art and engineering, craft and machine production, product design and manufacturing. Striking furniture, paintings, sculptures, objects, and (later) architecture resulted, envisaged as symbols of modernity. And the Bauhaus ethos went on to inspire numerous modern architects. By the 1930s, thanks partly to images produced there, curtain walls, flat roofs, corner windows, and apparently free-standing planes became linked together into what Reyner Banham later called 'the teenage uniform of modern architecture'.

Mies, on campus

The first of the four anointed superheroes of modern architecture I'll introduce here refined the logic of steel-framed architecture obsessively. Known to architects simply as 'Mies' (1886–1969), he was born Ludwig Mies at Aachen on the German–Dutch border. The family firm made stone fireplaces, and he acquired an early sense of the dignity of materials and the craftspeople who worked them. In 1922—spending time with artists from the Dada movement who deliberately cultivated their personas—he reinvented himself as Ludwig Mies van der Rohe, adding his mother's surname and the 'van der' which hinted (without basis) at Dutch nobility. Mies began his career as a draughtsman at the Berlin office of architect Peter Behrens from 1910–11, overlapping there with Gropius, Meyer, and, briefly, an odd Swiss man who later styled himself Le Corbusier.

Alongside his practical training, Mies read voraciously in philosophy, history, and art criticism, encouraged by the philosopher Alois Riehl who was an early client. Detlef Mertins has argued that Mies took from his apprenticeship with Behrens the idea of a quest for architectural forms, to suit the modern age, which could be seen as universal. From the work of Dutch architect H.P. Berlage, he became interested in a handful of so-called 'normal forms and types': basic shapes supposedly drawn from ancient traditions. From Gropius, Bruno Taut, and the so-called November Group, he took the idea that creativity, freedom, and social justice were connected. And, from Catholic philosopher Romano Guardini, he understood the purpose of life as directing the human spirit into the future. The resulting Mies was highly contradictory: a curious spiritual, non-political, socialist authoritarian. He was hard enough to place in interwar Germany that he was both commissioned to design a memorial to the murdered communists Karl Liebknecht and Rosa Luxembourg, 1926, and remained able to practice modern architecture after it was censured by the Nazis following their rise to power in 1933, until they decisively pronounced it 'degenerate' in 1937.

In that year, Mies was invited to design a house in the American state of Wyoming. His reputation preceded him, based on a pavilion he'd designed for a 1929 expo in Barcelona—a remarkable exercise in the architecture of planes—and on his role as the last head of the Bauhaus before it closed in 1933. On an extended visit, Mies negotiated an appointment as a professor with what became Illinois Institute of Technology (IIT) in Chicago, including a commission to masterplan its new campus at Bronzeville on the city's Near South Side. He thus became poised to bring together—in Chicago—European thinking about the steel frame as a symbol of modernity, with American talent for steel fabrication, in conjunction with the planar thinking previously cultivated by Wright, Gropius, and Rietveld.

Mies and his colleagues treated the IIT project like a scientific experiment. They sought a rational planning grid for the whole site, testing alternative geometries for combinations of laboratories, lecture theatres, and classrooms, eventually determining that a 7.3-metre grid could accommodate them all successfully. This grid was laid across the twelve-block site as a device for organizing individual buildings and the rooms inside them. The grid—symbolizing ideas of space and mathematical objectivity—reflected Mies's belief that the planning of buildings should be primarily a technical and rational exercise.

Over nearly fifteen years, Mies's office designed a sequence of low-rise rectangular blocks within IIT's grid. The first, a three-storey engineering lab—the Minerals and Metals Research Building, 1947—established the formula (Figure 6). Its primary structure was a welded steel frame on a regular module, expressed externally and internally, with special attention paid to the detailing of the corners. Echoing the Fagus factory, its steel frame was infilled with just two materials: glass 'curtains'—set in slender steel glazing bars—and panels of brickwork. To emphasize honestly that the brick was infill and not supporting structure, it was set forward from the frame as a visually separate plane. This assembly was topped with a flat roof hidden behind the steel capping beam, with hidden gutters. The façades were understood as a straightforward visual consequence of the spaces inside, and the means of construction. Windowless end elevations—a grid of welded steels and brick infill panels—were likened by Mies fans to the abstract modern paintings of Piet Mondrian.

Wishnick Hall, and Alumni Memorial Hall, 1946, and the Metallurgical and Chemical Engineering Building, 1947, tested variations of the formula, exploring different corner and capping

6. Minerals and Metals Research Building, Illinois Institute of Technology (IIT), Chicago, USA, 1947. The first in a sequence of buildings laid out on a grid on the IIT campus, seeking to perfect the ideal image for modern steel campus buildings. (Architect: Ludwig Mies van der Rohe.)

details, welding together combinations of I-section, rectangular hollow section, and flat plate steels to achieve subtly different effects. Extended through multiple projects at IIT, Mies's office engaged in the obsessive refinement of an architectural system, seeking to isolate ideal forms for campus buildings. Differences between successive buildings are barely discernible to non-specialists, but fans understood their development as a rigorous, spiritual quest to pare architecture down to basic forms and proportions. 'Less is more,' Mies proclaimed.

IIT's architecture school, S.R. Crown Hall, 1956 (Figure 7), is frequently acknowledged as the pinnacle of the group, although it's an exception, disobeying the grid, and owing less to its neighbours than a spectacular, if largely uninhabitable, house

7. S.R. Crown Hall, IIT, Chicago, USA, 1947. The exception that proved the rule on the IIT campus: an apparently hovering glass box, its supporting steel frame placed outside the walls, containing a single studio space, with 'servant spaces' in the basement below. Historians have understood it as a modern reinvention of the classical temple, poised above the ground on a plinth. (Architect: Ludwig Mies van der Rohe.)

designed by Mies's office for Edith Farnsworth at Plano, Illinois, 1951. That house was conceived as a glass-walled box almost hovering above the ground, its rooms subdivided only with furniture, with a supporting steel frame placed outside the walls. Crown Hall's fully glazed upper storey, like Farnsworth House, comprised a large single space, interrupted only by two stairs and a handful of timber screens. It sat on a half-buried basement containing a library, workshop, and teaching rooms, with the steel frame again placed outside the building, supporting a secondary order of smaller steels holding the glazing.

Crown Hall was a modern abstraction of a classical Greek temple, with a stepped base, columns, and intricately judged proportions. Its single studio room symbolized rational modern space. That room's ceiling—dropped to hide the upper glazing bars of the perimeter window frames—was inscribed with a grid, seemingly extending into the infinite distance. The glass walls were clear at the top and obscured with milky film below, focusing the students' view on the sky and trees—understood as universal symbols of the natural world—rather than the messiness of passers-by. The fact of so many students sharing a large room, their desks arranged in orderly rows, produced a monastic calm where Mies's curriculum was obsessively pursued. Some saw the studio as a blank canvas accentuating the vibrancy of human life within. Others understood its abstract qualities, and its tendency to make its inhabitants self-police their behaviour, as rigid and autocratic.

It's seldom done in histories of modern architecture to note that the exposed steelwork of Mies's IIT buildings, paired with thin brickwork panels and single-glazed windows, made the buildings perishingly cold in Chicago's freezing winters, and unbearably hot in summer. It's also rare to mention that, because steel and brickwork expand and contract at different rates, many brick panels cracked, and flat roofs, hidden behind steel for visual effect, regularly leaked. For Mies fans—like the admirers of other famous modern architects—these were merely defensible consequences of genius.

Until recently, architectural histories also rarely acknowledged that the blocks over which Mies laid his planning grid were no empty lot. They were cleared as slums by the largely white city and Institute authorities in the 1940s, having previously housed a notable middle-class black community whose cultural life was expressed in a vibrant jazz scene. Some have reinterpreted their demolition as racially motivated social cleansing. Historian Tim Samuelson has illustrated how the Mecca Apartments, a welcoming home for black immigrants to Chicago, immortalized in the Mecca Flat Blues (1924), was cleared to make way for Crown Hall. An alternative interpretation of Mies's campus planning grid is thus possible here—in conjunction with interpretations of Crown Hall as autocratic—not just as a symbol of technical objectivity but also as a symbol of authoritarian power.

Mies in the sky

Mies's talent for making architectural images in steel was strikingly demonstrated by his office's high-rise buildings from the 1950s and 1960s. These drew inspiration from an early project.

In 1921, Mies entered an architectural competition for a site on Friedrichstrasse in Berlin with a design for a skyscraper. He made two striking photomontages celebrating the literal transparency of all-glass façades: one showing floor to ceiling glazing enigmatically reflecting the sky in daylight; the other illustrating its see-through qualities when lit from within at night. Although they didn't win Mies the competition, these images later became famous, anticipating the modern tower block.

The first steel towers built to the designs of Mies's office were twin apartment blocks overlooking Lake Michigan, turned at 90 degrees to each other, connected with a slender low-level canopy, known as 860–880 Lake Shore Drive. Internal 'cores' provided the buildings' structural stability, accommodating the elevators and vertical services. Individual flats, eight per floor, were laid out around the cores, designed as open spaces, with fitted furniture and sliding screens substituting for most walls and doors.

Structurally, a grid of primary steel columns was placed inside the outer edges of the towers' floors, encased in concrete for fireproofing. Prefabricated secondary steel elements were then fixed to the façade, expressed as vertical I-sections, four per structural bay. These steels supported aluminium-framed windows and provided so-called lateral bracing, reinforcing the building against wind loads. A small break in the secondary steels at every floor level illustrated visually on the façade that these secondary steels weren't continuous, and therefore weren't primary supports for the building. But, to the consternation of Mies fans, every fifth I-section was fitted directly over a concrete-encased primary steel column. These steels thus had no structural purpose, added instead to maintain the rhythm of the façade. For good modernists accustomed to Mies's dictum that 'less is more', and Sullivan's 'form ever follows function', these steels remained unnecessary. They were functionally redundant adornments, serving only the visual image of the tower, and they became objects of controversy among modern architects.

Just as Mies imagined the Minerals and Metals Building as a prototype for campus architecture, Lake Shore Drive was envisaged as a prototype for steel-framed towers. The formula was refined in a series of projects accommodating diverse functions: further apartments on Commonwealth Promenade in Chicago, 1956; courtrooms at the Dirksen Federal Building in Chicago's Loop, 1964; and offices for distillers Seagram in New York, 1958. The same elements recurred: 'shell-and-core' planning (an internal core containing services and elevators, surrounded by floorplates), and 'curtain' façades characterized by I-section steels.

The Seagram building, designed with Philip Johnson, was a refined and expensive variation on the theme (Figure 8). Liquor baron Samuel Bronfman, the client, was egged on by his daughter, Phyllis Lambert, who trained as an architect at IIT. Rather than stepping back from the street like most New York skyscrapers, maximizing the building's volume within strict zoning laws,

---

8. **Seagram Building, New York, USA, 1958. A 'shell and core' tower with 'curtain' walls, characterized by I-section columns, providing office space for a firm of distillers. It was a key building in its architect's sequence of architectural experiments to find the ideal form for the modern tower. Both typical and exceptional, it is both a refined building for a specific client on a specific site, and a universal symbol of corporate modernity, imitated globally. (Architect: Ludwig Mies van der Rohe.)**

Iron and steel

Seagram was a straightforward rectangular block. Façade I-sections were special castings in bronze rather than stock steel sections. Key interior surfaces were clad in marble and travertine. A band of artificial lighting around the perimeter of each ceiling heightened the drama of the building's stacked floorplates when seen from below at night. Glazed internal office partitions were designed to emphasize the open plan layout. Venetian blinds were fitted with only three settings—open, closed, and half-closed—to present an orderly image to the street. A modern art programme commissioned murals, tapestries, and canvases from luminaries including Pablo Picasso and Mark Rothko. And a plain granite plaza outside, lifted three steps from the street, made a calm garden. Seagram became *the* archetypal steel and glass tower. It became both typical and exceptional: a refined building for a specific client on a specific site, and simultaneously a universal symbol of corporate modernity, imitated worldwide.

The details of Mies's towers—like columns placed for visual effect as cladding over structural ones, and decorative steel casings fitted around structural columns—didn't always express their structural logic directly. But they did always illustrate its idea. Mies's towers, like most modern buildings were 'representational': they didn't represent ideas about the past like previous architectures had, but engaged instead in self-representation, expressing—and sometimes subtly enhancing—the imagery of their own constructional logic to evoke ideas about modernity.

Shaping modern culture in steel

In 1831, Victor Hugo had anticipated a modern architecture reflecting scientific culture, arguing for special buildings, which people could identify with as symbols of the age. Mies believed that his work fulfilled this promise. Indeed, his fans likened the I-section steels of Lake Shore Drive to the tracery of medieval Gothic cathedrals. 'True architecture,' Mies claimed, 'is always objective and is the expression of the inner structure of our times, from which it comes'. He didn't just think he was designing individual buildings for individual sites and clients. He thought he was isolating the universal forms of architecture itself, paring down the logic of steel—and building types like campus buildings and high-rise towers—to their essential images. Mies imagined himself not as inventing a style, but as identifying *the* authentic, timeless architectural expression of the future. Once the job of isolating these forms was done, Mies imagined he would pass the images and techniques to others for repeating and refining. He imagined he was designing bespoke prototypes for others to mass produce. Indeed, he lavished attention on the first campus buildings and towers designed in his office but—once he felt the archetypes were established—left later versions to his associates.

Easily imagined as a kit of columns and beams, like the construction toy Meccano, iron and steel nurtured ideas about a perfected modern architecture. Philosopher Walter Benjamin noted in 1935 how the imagery of iron architecture was derived 'dialectically' out of the conflict between old symbolic codes developed for stone and wood, and new forms of structural technology. Iron and steel frames encouraged the integration of structure with services, and ideas of 'space' with industrial production, assembling buildings from sophisticated engineered components to express ideas about technological modernity. The emphasis on the rational structural calculation of components shifted design attention from the whole building to the part, just as scientific cultures shifted Western thinking from traditional holistic religious views to a greater focus on the individual. Such shifts were as latent in the Iron Bridge and Eiffel Tower as they were at Crown Hall and Seagram. The job of the architect-genius, as Mies 'modestly' understood himself in later life, was to work through the cultural and social consequences of new logics of production, to determine the true architectural forms of modernity. For him, the material best suited to those labours was steel.

Chapter 3
Reinforced concrete

Reinforced concrete and the sale of expertise

The reinforced concrete entrepreneur François Hennebique designed a four-storey villa for his family in the Parisian suburb of Bourg-la-Reine in 1904 (Figure 9), demonstrating his firm's talents with the material that made his fortune. Architectural critics were snobbish about the house's eccentricities, but it remains an object of fascination because of Hennebique's global domination of reinforced concrete construction at the start of the 20th century.

Reinforced concrete lends itself to a structural form called the cantilever—where a slab or beam is hung outwards from one side, suspended without columns, counter-weighted by a mass of structure behind. The Hennebique villa incorporated every kind of cantilever possible at that time. Its floors stepped down to the rear as a series of terraces, covered with soil and densely planted as 'hanging gardens', illustrating concrete's substantial load-bearing capacity. By contrast, the terrace balustrades showed how delicate concrete elements could become. Looming above the house, cantilevered out from it, was a sculptural concrete water tower, which neighbours nicknamed 'the minaret'. The villa's external walls followed an innovative construction method, where concrete was poured in situ between 3-centimetre-thick

9. Villa Hennebique, Bourg-la-Reine, Paris, France, 1904. A show-off house designed by an entrepreneur for his family, displaying novel uses for reinforced concrete. It reflected Hennebique's global domination of reinforced concrete construction at the beginning of the 20th century. (Designer: François Hennebique.)

precast concrete slabs. These slabs provided permanent formwork for structural concrete poured in behind, replacing the sacrificial timber shuttering normally used to make temporary moulds for concrete construction. They served to conceal the concrete poured on site, whose finish could be unreliable, giving a more reliable precast finish, and were hand tooled to reveal the flint aggregate used in the mix, so they looked like stone from a distance.

Hennebique didn't invent reinforced concrete but commercialized it ingeniously. The ancient Romans had used concrete 2,000 years before, working out how to make mortar by mixing kiln-dried lime with sand and water, adding stone dust to produce a paste that set hard when it dried in the air. They subsequently found that, by adding a natural compound of iron oxide and silica alumina, mortar could harden in large quantities independently of the air. We now call this cement. Large quantities of cement poured around broken bricks and fragments of stone were employed to make the first concrete walls in Rome in the 2nd century BCE (although the name concrete, describing cement combined with masonry aggregate, didn't emerge until the 19th century). The most significant Roman invention—when concrete started to find its own architectural logic—was the vaulted concrete floor, an important invention for the Roman empire because of its scarcity of timber. And the most spectacular survival of Roman concrete is the soaring dome of the Pantheon in Rome, (probably) completed in 125 CE.

Historically, concrete was strong in compression but poor in tension. It proved itself as a material for walls, vaults, and domes—which carry loads in compression—but not for beams and spans—reliant on tension. And because the outcome of each concrete pour could be temperamental, depending on the precise mix, the temperature and humidity when it was poured, as well as the builder's skill in achieving a reliable outcome, concrete wasn't widely used between Roman and Victorian times.

The structures required by 19th-century industries and infrastructures revived interest in concrete, however. As skills in working the material gradually improved, inventors tried combining it with iron. Iron was stronger in tension but weaker in compression—the opposite properties to concrete—and the combination of materials held promise. In 1854, a plasterer called William Boutland Wilkinson from Newcastle-upon-Tyne, UK, patented a method for inserting iron barrel hoops as tension rods at the crown of concrete vaults. In 1875, William Henry Lascelles, a London building contractor, filed a patent for strengthening concrete panels with iron rods, and strengthening concrete floors with wire mesh. In 1877, Thaddeus Hyatt, a New York manufacturer, published an account of fifteen years' experimentation with reinforced concrete, establishing that iron reinforcement added to the bottom of a concrete beam would cope with tension, while concrete at the top would handle compression, countering what engineers call 'bending moments' to produce rigid structural elements. He also established that iron covered with concrete would remain undamaged in fire, promoting 'ferro-concrete' as a fireproof material. Experiments and patents multiplied towards the end of the 19th century.

Hennebique's own innovations weren't extraordinary. He substituted steel reinforcement for iron, and spaced steel straps closer together near the ends of beams where structural loads were greater. It was his patents filed in 1892, however, that established his fortune. His genius lay in recognizing the commercial opportunities those patents established. As soon as they were signed, Hennebique sold his contracting concern and established a reinforced concrete construction consultancy. It provided engineering drafting services, licensing only reliable contractors to construct its designs. And it guarded its intellectual property jealously, challenging infringements with legal action. In 1892, the Hennebique firm employed two engineer-draughtsmen in Paris, growing by 1894 to fifty-six engineers supplying drawings to fifty-five licensed contractors, and by 1909 to sixty-two drafting offices around the world. If a client wanted a steel-reinforced concrete-framed building at the beginning of the 20th century, they had little choice but to use a patented system, among which Hennebique's was most prominent. The firm's magazine *Le Beton Armé* (*Reinforced Concrete*) promoted its technical expertise and extended concrete's aura of innovation. Hennebique thus established the idea of the professional construction consultancy, which was as important to the emergence of modern architecture as any of the buildings discussed in this book.

Hennebique's house thus indicated how reinforced concrete could symbolize the new, prefiguring the emergence of a technically oriented construction industry. It anticipated the higher status and value that gradually became accorded to design skills over craft skills. It also illustrates how entrepreneurial modern architects and engineers learnt they could monetize intellectual property and professional expertise—be it technical prowess or visual innovation—as much as designing buildings.

Ethics of production and living

Beginning as a gloopy liquid but setting hard, reinforced concrete is a troublesome commodity. In philosophy, 'concrete' refers to something immediately present. However, as Adrian Forty has shown, many thinkers have struggled with the contradictory qualities of this demanding material. Famous for making dramatic forms, concrete has no form of its own, merely shaped by the formwork into which it is poured. Seemingly substantial, cement only becomes strong when combined with aggregate and steel. While the ingredients of concrete are natural, it grew to symbolize the human-made world. And, while it's been imagined as timeless, concrete frequently came to represent the new because of its difference from other materials. It was attributed a moral rightness because its finished surfaces bear 'honest' traces of how they were worked. Less legible than steel's kit of parts, however, concrete became a curious architectural symbol of technological modernity.

American architect Albert Kahn matched François Hennebique for commercial nous, remarking that 'architecture is 90% business and 10% art'. His office, mixing architects and engineers, designed no-nonsense buildings for industry, developing early expertise in reinforced concrete. Concrete stood for an ethic of production in the early factories his organization designed.

In 1909, Kahn's office designed the Automobile Assembly Building for motorcar pioneer Henry Ford's Highland Park plant in Detroit, Michigan (Figure 10). It was laid out around the production line for Ford's 'Model T'; the vehicle, produced between 1908 and

10. Automobile Assembly Building, Highland Park, Detroit, USA, 1909. A reinforced concrete-framed factory laid out around the production line for Henry Ford's famous 'Model T' car. It illustrated Ford's capitalism: his theories about the methodical process of goods through a workshop, the consignment of tasks to individual workers, and the technical analysis of processes to identify efficiencies. (Architect: Albert Kahn.)

1927, which opened up motoring to ordinary Americans. Early cars were made using traditional coachbuilding techniques, where the vehicle stayed in one place, worked on by a sequence of skilled trades. Ford instead refined a method of keeping trades and machines static while cars moved between them, calculating assembly processes around the space needed for each task and the time taken to execute it—which became elevated into the so-called Fordist theory of industrial production. Ford's thinking promoted the methodical process of goods through a workshop and the consignment of tasks to individual workers, rather than relying on their initiative, promoting the rational analysis of processes to identify efficiencies.

Kahn and Ford shared ideas, becoming friends, and the Highland Park factory can be understood as a built diagram of their thinking together. It comprised a four-storey concrete frame, relatively long and thin, with decoration limited to an ornamented cornice. Internally, there were no dividing walls. Vertical circulation and staff changing spaces were pushed outside the primary volume, as towers, to maximize continuous space for machinery. The concrete frame was infilled externally with floor to ceiling glazing, maximizing light. Gravity was used to shift parts from upper floors to the main production line at ground level, and cars moved along this production line with components dropped onto them from above. Car bodies, for example, complete with doors and seats, were slid down chutes for fitting to their chassis. If the processes on each floor were properly coordinated, Ford believed, lazy working would become immediately apparent. Architecturally, Highland Park was transitional, with origins in 18th-century European mill buildings that had separate workshops on multiple floors. And Kahn's later factories for Ford—like the River Rouge plant in Detroit—became even clearer diagrams of industrial processes, concentrating production into a single line on a single floor.

Concrete came to stand for Fordist industrial production in Detroit, representing capitalist free enterprise, the efficiency of centralized industry, dedication to work, and self-sacrifice. However, it could also stand for socialist collective living. Twenty years after Highland Park, in 1929, the Narkomfin Communal House was completed in Moscow to designs by architects Moisei Ginzburg and Ignatii Milinis (Figure 11). The Russian Revolution of 1917 had overturned the autocratic regime of the Tsar and—inspired by communist ideas of Karl Marx and Friedrich Engels—ousted the so-called bourgeois class of aristocrats and managers in favour of worker's councils called Soviets. By the time that the Narkomfin was constructed, there was a drive to industrialize the Soviet economy, paralleled by a cultural revolution seeking to restructure social life along Marxist lines.

Commissioned as a prototype, the Narkomfin was a radical exercise in social engineering. Designed for bureaucrats of the Ministry of

11. **Narkomfin Communal House, Moscow, Russia, 1929. A radical experiment in communist social engineering: a 'social condenser' housing bureaucrats of the Ministry of Finance, including twenty-four collectivized flats whose residents ate, relaxed, and socialized together, imagined as sharing ideals and daily practicalities. (Architects: Moisei Ginzburg and Ignatii Milinis.)**

Finance, it replaced two bourgeois villas on Moscow's Garden Ring Road. Dressed in modern architecture's Gropius-inspired 'teenage uniform', it boasted white painted concrete walls with flat roofs and ribbon windows, seemingly hovering above the ground on columns. It was most striking for its radical organization. Devised by a state research agency headed by Ginzburg, it maximized shared facilities, like those for cooking and dining, adding a library, gymnasium, and laundry, plus a crèche with professional childcare so women could play a fuller role in society. The flats were grouped into a single slab, connected with a bridge to another block containing most of the communal spaces, while a laundry and crèche stood as separate buildings in the garden. The aim was to socialize private aspects of domestic life into the public sphere.

Different flat types were included. Two so-called 'transitional' flats weren't dependent on communal facilities. However, twenty-four 'collectivized' units were provided for individuals or couples: compact double-height volumes, accommodating only sleeping, showers, and toilets. These had no kitchens, and living space was minimal, because residents were expected to spend most of their home lives as part of the collective—eating, relaxing, and exercising together—sharing ideals and daily practicalities.

The Narkomfin was never the fully communal society its champions envisaged because of the multiple flat types. Indeed, a rooftop penthouse was added at a late stage for the minister of finance, separate from the collective, and Ginzburg added an enlarged version of the 'transitional' unit for himself. Moreover, the prototype was barely repeated because Soviet communism changed around it. The Narkomfin was celebrated in 1928, but Stalinist authorities declared by 1930 that workers preferred conventional domestic arrangements, and Ginzburg was required to disown the building as an elitist experiment.

Together, the Narkomfin and Highland Park show how concrete structures came to stand for radically opposing ideas of communism and high capitalism in the 20th century. They indicate how concrete—at once liquid and solid, formless and formed, natural and human-made—became associated with divergent attempts to rethink social order and mechanized production. They illustrate how the material was not only contradictory in itself, but also had divergent ideas about modernity projected onto it.

Inventing Le Corbusier

The second superhero of modern architecture I'll introduce was an intense French-speaking Swiss man, Charles-Edouard Jeanneret (1887–1965), who wrestled with reinforced concrete as a way of wrestling with what architecture could do. He moved to Paris in 1917, after art school, and after designing a series of almost-modern houses in his hometown of La Chaux-de-Fonds. He painted together with the artist Amédée Ozenfant (whose family knew the Hennebiques) and they labelled themselves 'purists', publishing an art manifesto together, *After Cubism*, 1918, demanding a reclamation of order after the fragmentation of Cubism. They depicted everyday objects in flattened compositions, borrowing projection techniques from engineering drawing. Jeanneret reinvented his architecture and himself, becoming 'Le Corbusier'—combining a historic family surname, Le Corbesier, with the French word for raven, *corbeau*, a haughty bird he thought he looked like—believing that, by doing so, he was identifying himself with the deep origins of human civilization.

Flora Samuel has observed that concrete was, for Corbusier, a natural material, and he imagined being under concrete as being cocooned within the earth. He was as contradictory as the material itself. He took himself very seriously but was mercilessly self-mocking. He celebrated the straightforwardness of technology and the 'engineer's aesthetic', but designed with a painter's instinct for form, colour, and proportion. He rejected symmetry but employed it selectively. He praised the machine age while believing—as William Curtis put it—in 'an equilibrium between the mechanized and the rustic, the secular and the sacred [and] the local and the universal'. His thinking blended practicality with a yearning for primeval mysticism. He identified modernity as the source of *The New Spirit* (the name of a magazine he co-published with Ozenfant in the 1920s), seeking inspiration from history, understanding pure geometries—the cylinder, pyramid, cube, block, and sphere—as the true inheritance of the classical past, claiming architecture to be 'the magnificent, knowledgeable and correct play of volumes under light'. Corbusier employed a substantial studio but was quick to claim his own genius, believing himself—in the terms of Friedrich Nietzsche, the philosopher of destiny—one of a select group of 'world historical individuals'. When devotees copied his architecture, he reinvented it. Condemned as a villain for his ideas on urban planning, Corbusier nevertheless remains a hero for his buildings, which significantly extended architecture's organizational and expressive potential.

The late 1910s and 1920s saw major technological and cultural achievements in Europe and America. These followed a rush for technical advantage during the First World War, and responded to its horrors. Movements in modern art were matched by modern novelists 'making it new' like Virginia Woolf, James Joyce, and Marcel Proust. Meanwhile, cultural theorists like Walter Benjamin and Siegfried Kracauer tried to account for the experiences of modern life, especially the alienation they believed it produced. Increasing dissemination of still photography paralleled a cinema boom which made moving, and then talking, pictures widespread. Radio and gramophones brought news and entertainment into prosperous homes. Glamorous ocean liners made international shipping faster and more luxurious. Motor cars were an increasingly regular sight. Air travel became possible for the rich, and daring pioneer aviators became newsworthy. Medical innovations like penicillin and insulin seemed poised to transform public health, which became a prominent preoccupation. And the emergence of jazz and swing was matched with waltz, polka, and twostep. As the 1920s drew to a close, a recognizable cultural and technological 'avant garde' was emerging, and it started forming public opinion.

A house begun in 1928 and finished in 1931—Villa Savoye, at Poissy, outside Paris—is sometimes portrayed as the definitive architectural reflection of the jazz age. The architecture of planes lent itself more logically to reinforced concrete than steel for Corbusier, and Villa Savoye fulfilled a series of his early experiments. Corbusier's planar compositions related to, but differed from, Wright's and Rietveld's, in which walls and furniture elements 'pinwheeled' outwards from a centre, being contained instead within boxes. Villa Savoye extended ideas that were first explored in an unbuilt house project—Maison Citrohan, 1922, intended for mass production like France's Citröen car, famously promoted as a 'machine for living'—which were then tested in a sequence of houses around Paris, co-designed with Corbusier's cousin Pierre Jeanneret, including: Maison La Roche-Jeanneret, 1924; Maison Cook, 1926; and Villa Stein-de-Monzie, 1928. Villa Savoye was never a good house to live in, frequently cold and damp, and it became a ruin after the Savoye family were deported by the Nazis in the Second World War. But its image proved long-lasting enough that the French government eventually restored it as a cultural treasure.

Villa Savoye was constructed in concrete frame infilled with blockwork and tile, rendered-over and painted white to give the impression of continuous concrete planes (Figure 12). Perched on a ridge in a rolling landscape, it's almost square in plan. First-floor living spaces apparently float above the ground on a column grid. Recessed beneath, painted dark green to emphasize the floating illusion, the ground floor is shaped around the turning circle of a car—that definitive mass-produced symbol of modern life. The column grid is almost, but not quite, regular, with a few

12. Villa Savoye, Poissy, France, 1931. It was a built in a concrete frame infilled with blockwork and tile, rendered-over and painted white to give the impression of continuous concrete planes. Its first-floor living spaces apparently float above a recessed ground floor shaped around the turning circle of a car—that mass-produced symbol of modern life. Arguably the definitive image of the modern house, it has been much interpreted. (Architects: Le Corbusier and Pierre Jeanneret.)

columns artfully shifted off-grid. The grid thus establishes the house's rational credentials, while its rogue columns simultaneously highlight its artfulness.

After being deposited by their chauffeur, the Savoyes entered the lobby, enclosed floor to ceiling with industrial glazing, as reminiscent of a factory as of a house. A washbasin was placed here symbolically. It had multiple meanings, standing for: the modern preoccupation with health and hygiene; the holy water stoop placed at the door of Catholic churches; and the urinal that artist René Duchamp displayed controversially in an art gallery in 1917, entitled 'Fountain', and claimed as a 'readymade' 'object-type' as culturally significant as any artwork. From here, the Savoyes ascended a steep ramp cut through the centre of the house to reach the first floor. This storey appeared solid from the outside—characterized by a horizontal strip of windows running around all four elevations—but it was partly hollowed out to provide an open sundeck accessed from the living spaces and bedrooms. The appearance of solidity was maintained because the façades, and their window strips, sailed across the front of the deck. The house's living spaces were strikingly light-filled in comparison to conventional masonry buildings. Finishes blended industrial and domestic imagery, evoking the decks of ocean liners and train interiors. The bathroom associated with the master bedroom was expressed as a shrine to cleanliness and 'primitiveness', centred on a sinuous recliner for naked relaxation.

The second flight of the ramp led to a roof terrace with a highly modelled enclosing wall. Notionally a windbreak, this curved plane served a primarily sculptural purpose when seen from outside, as a cylinder placed artfully above the rectangle of the first floor.

There are as many interpretations of Villa Savoye as there are numerous academic texts about it. It's been seen as a fulfilment of two formulas for modern architecture promoted by Corbusier in the 1920s. The first was the cinematic idea of 'architectural promenade'—extending Schmarsow's theories, and discussed in Corbusier's 1923 book *Towards a New Architecture*—claiming that space is primarily appreciated by moving around it. In this context, Villa Savoye's ramp can be understood as a promenade device, unfolding the house's sequence of rooms. The second formula it exemplified was Corbusier's 'five points for a new architecture', published in *The New Spirit* in 1926, attempting a scientific categorization of modern architecture's 'teenage uniform' into key elements:

1. The replacement of loadbearing masonry walls with a grid of reinforced concrete columns, called *piloti*;
2. The free plan, imagining walls as planes in space liberated from their structural function by interior columns;

3. The free façade, recognizing that structural columns liberate elevations from bearing loads;
4. The horizontal window, made possible because non-loadbearing elevations allow openings to be placed differently, supposedly lighting rooms evenly, and;
5. Roof gardens, compensating for the green space that a building consumes by replacing it on top as a flat roof.

Villa Savoye exemplified these points. Perched on *piloti*, with its roof garden highlighted by the sculptural windbreak, its columns were conspicuously detached from the walls, illustrating the 'free plan'. And the horizontal window strips emphasized how the walls above didn't transfer their loads to the ground but instead to the columns behind. Although Corbusier later moved away from these 'five points', architecture students love a formula, and they've remained doggedly persistent.

Villa Savoye has also been read as a ship, a machine, an Arcadian landscape, a macho fantasy, and a bourgeois villa in socialist clothing. Others have seen it as a reinvention of a Greek temple: sat on a hilltop, with its façade divided—like temple fronts—into three parts, with elevations judiciously proportioned (according to a system Corbusier devised called 'regulating lines'). Like the ritual route to a temple's sanctuary, climbing Villa Savoye's ramp has been seen as symbolizing an ascent to the gods. The critic Sigfried Giedion emphasized that the house coincided with the increasing acceptance of Albert Einstein's theories of relativity—published in 1905 and 1916—reimagining space and time as a single interdependent continuum. Giedion linked architectural promenade—imagining buildings as experiences unfolded in space and time—to relativity, as an illustration of the idea of time being inseparable from space. Later historians, interested in theories of the body, emphasized instead the cleanliness demanded by the house, and its fixation with the naked figure.

Commentaries on Villa Savoye were conducted in building as well as writing. Although Irish designer Eileen Gray's house E.1027 was finished before Villa Savoye, in 1929, she knew it from prepublished drawings. E.1027 was an alphabetic code combining Gray's name with that of her collaborator Jean Badovici, editor of the magazine *Living Architecture*. Built for their use together, perched above the sea at Roquebrune-Cap-Martin near Monaco, the house initially subscribes to the 'five points' (Figure 13). It was lifted on *piloti* with ribbon windows, a roof garden, and internal walls expressed as planes detached from structural concrete columns. But Gray challenged Corbusier's work: the image of hygiene 'to bore you to death', and the 'poverty' of modern architecture stemming 'from the atrophy of sensuality'. E.1027

13. **E.1027, Roquebrune-Cap-Martin, France, 1929. Combining elements from Villa Savoye and the Schröder House, this villa was more mature than both: a striking image of architectural function fitted intimately to the micro-rituals of daily life. Light and shadow were thoughtfully composed, with windows located to frame views when inhabitants stood or sat in certain places. (Architect: Eileen Gray.)**

was intimately tuned to its inhabitants, its bespoke furniture choreographing daily life. Materials were chosen to enhance how the building was touched. Cupboards were tailored around their contents, selectively hidden or revealed. Light fittings and radiators were integrated thoughtfully. Gray designed a gramophone trolley that could be wheeled outside, another with a cork surface to stop tea cups rattling, plus special chairs—some soft, some hard—for particular purposes. Light and shadow were thoughtfully composed, and windows were located to frame views when inhabitants stood or sat in certain places. Combining elements from Villa Savoye and the Schröder House, E.1027 was more mature than both: a striking image of architectural function fitted intimately to the micro-rituals of daily life. The historian Beatriz Colomina has suggested that Corbusier visited and was jealous, struggling to accept that a woman designed such an accomplished modern house. Staying there in 1938, after Gray moved out, he exacted weird psychological revenge, Colomina argued, daubing eight murals depicting sexualized female figures which changed E.1027's character by dematerializing certain planes visually: an act understood as vandalism.

Other critiques of Villa Savoye included, in the 1980s, a series of houses obsessively designed by architect Peter Eisenman around variations of grid and promenade. In 2001, the Australian practice ARM collaged a distorted *black* replica of the Villa Savoye into the Institute of Aboriginal and Torres Strait Islander Studies in Canberra, to make a point about Western colonists' emasculation of indigenous traditions.

Some historians portrayed the planar white houses of early modern architecture as stark and banal: as crude functionalism. But the artistry of Villa Savoye and E.1027 illustrate how this argument is simplistic. Their imagery drew from supposedly everyday functional artefacts: aeroplanes, boats, trains, cars, and factories. But they also simultaneously manipulated and heightened those images, appreciating their significance as talismans of the age, reinventing them in architecture to advocate that high culture should embrace global modernity.

The International Style

By the 1930s, enough buildings had been built with enough in common for critics to claim a distinctive modern architecture. Two influential books set out genealogies, or studies in family resemblance.

The International Style, published in 1932, catalogued an exhibition at New York's Museum of Modern Art (MoMA), presenting photographs and plans of buildings that more or less complied with Corbusier's 'five points'. His work was shown alongside that of Mies and Gropius, their reputations only emerging at that time. Other buildings given comparable emphasis were designed by architects who became less effective self-publicists and have been largely forgotten including: Uno Åhren, Ludwig Kysela, J.J.P Oud, Lily Reich (the only woman), Nicolaiev & Fissenko, and Manora Yamada. The show emerged from European road trips taken by MoMA's director Alfred Barr with critic Henry-Russell Hitchcock and a history graduate, Philip Johnson (who later retrained as an architect and collaborated with Mies on the Seagram offices).

Barr, Hitchcock, and Johnson argued that the buildings they depicted shared an aesthetic resemblance. They presented them as progenitors of a distinctive architectural *style*. Style in architecture was effectively a 19th-century idea, popularized by German writer Alois Riegel. It described a predominantly visual approach to buildings where certain shapes and forms characterize the architectures of particular historical epochs—no matter that individual buildings get produced in different places at different times by different people under different social, cultural, and political conditions. 'Classical', 'Baroque', 'Gothic', and 'Gothic Revival' styles have been defined, for example, spanning extensive time periods and geographies. Styles are thus ideas projected back onto architectures of the past by historians. *The International Style* claimed modern architecture as a style like other styles, characterizing it as functional, following three principles:

> [an] emphasis on volume—space enclosed by thin planes or surfaces as opposed to the suggestion of mass and solidity; regularity as opposed to symmetry or other kinds of obvious balance; and, lastly, dependence on the intrinsic elegance of materials, technical perfection and fine proportions, as opposed to applied ornament.

The idea that modern architecture could be depicted as a style was disputed by establishment architects of the time, who subscribed to older styles, offended by what they saw as modernism's blunt crudeness. Modern architects, on the other hand, disliked the show's emphasis on aesthetics over function, thinking it over-simplified their work, believing instead that their designs demonstrated timeless technical and social principles. Indeed, they suspected that characterizing modern architecture as a style sowed the seeds of its destruction, making it transitory, opening up space for something else to follow.

Art historian Nikolaus Pevsner arrived in Britain from Germany shortly after MoMA's show, sacked from Göttingen University by the Nazis for his Jewishness. He brought enthusiasm for modernism—which he understood as the true architectural expression of the age—and a desire to promote it to a sceptical British public, reflected in his book *The Pioneers of Modern Architecture: From William Morris to Walter Gropius*, 1936. Pevsner's story located the origins of modernism in the art theories of William Morris and John Ruskin—who examined how mechanized industry was changing society, and argued that art and architecture should change in response. Pevsner identified provisional responses to this problem in the flowing, naturally inspired shapes of Art Nouveau and the so-called Arts and Crafts movement led by Morris—which sought to return to the handmade crafts of preindustrial architecture—and also in 19th-century engineering structures like railway sheds. But these were only transitional responses to industrialization, Pevsner argued, either rejecting modernity's consequences or failing to understand the full implications of industrial production. Only in the work of Gropius and the Bauhaus, he argued—in buildings like those collected in *The International Style*—had the proper architectural expression of modernity been achieved. Although they didn't get on, Barr, Hitchcock, and Johnson saw how Pevsner was reinforcing modern architecture by equipping it with a history and, in 1942, MoMA republished an expanded edition of his book retitled *The Pioneers of Modern Design*.

These influential texts gave modern architecture momentum in the 1930s and 1940s. But they also over-simplified it. They admitted modernism into the realm of high culture, but only through a 19th-century, premodern idea of architectural history as a sequence of visual styles. Nevertheless, the arguments of these books became so pervasive that they continue to shape how modern architecture remains understood.

Cities of tomorrow

Modernity transformed Western cities through industrialization in the 19th and early 20th centuries. Populations shifted from agricultural labour to industrial production, from dispersal on the land to concentrations around new work in offices and factories. Established cities grew substantially, and more were built. Much of this growth was unplanned and opportunistic, driven by market forces and short-term necessities. Early industrial cities were frequently characterized by cramped living conditions, polluted air and water, little sanitation, bad health and hygiene, poor sunlight, and a lack of green space. Infrastructures were often provided only in retrospect—railways, for example, retrofitted to shift goods and commuters, or paved roads to accommodate motor traffic—choking urban life and public space. City 'slums' became widely condemned, often by well-to-do philanthropists who associated bad conditions with moral depravity among the poor. Improvements were demanded, and the gradual provision of sewers, water, gas, and electricity infrastructures transformed city life. But their installation was often piecemeal and disruptive, highlighting a lack of organized planning for urban growth.

Around the turn of the 20th century, various ideal city layouts were proposed, speculating about how cities could be planned for the machine age, how urban space might be different if organized properly around the new infrastructures. They coincided with the emergence of town planning as a profession, out of a long tradition of planned cities, spanning from the symbolic grid of historic Beijing, and the axes of Ancient Rome, to the crescents and circuses of Georgian Bath; from the boulevards cut through 19th-century Paris by Baron Haussmann to the gridirons of Manhattan and Chicago.

British inventor Ebeneezer Howard published a proposal for 'Garden Cities of To-morrow' in 1898, inspired by ideas about social reform and the authenticity of nature. He envisaged circular-plan 'slumless, smokeless' towns of 32,000 people dispersed across an agricultural landscape, supposedly combining the best of town and country. Industry, retail, and residential areas would be separated into concentric zones to promote public health. No Garden Cities were built following Howard's formula, but some 'garden villages' and 'garden suburbs' were constructed in the 1910s, comprising picturesque cottages with gardens, designed by Arts and Crafts architects. Their romantic imagery was later exploited by property developers in the 1920s and '30s who mass produced cheap copies as suburban sprawl. Howard's Garden City prompted Frank Lloyd Wright's speculative Broadacre City proposal for the USA, 1932: a car-oriented, low-density vision giving each family an acre of land for a house and smallholding, revisited during the Cold War for its potential to disperse the American population against the threat of nuclear attack.

Notoriously, Corbusier's studio also produced a sequence of speculative ideal city designs. His (unbuilt) Ville Contemporaine, or Contemporary City, 1922, fused the philanthropic ambitions of the Garden City with the formal axes of Haussman's Paris and the grids of Manhattan and Chicago. Ville Contemporaine proposed a new form of community. Its key functions were to be concentrated into cruciform towers built from mass-produced parts. A grid of highways would enclose these towers, freeing up land in between for parks, celebrating the health-giving potential of sunlight and fresh air in contrast to 19th-century density and pollution, echoing Ruskin's ideas about the moral importance of nature. Traffic was to be separated from pedestrians, with urban motorways divided from pedestrian routes through green space. The centre of Ville Contemporaine would comprise a seven-level road-rail interchange topped with an airport. Its innovations were vertical rather than horizontal, its section orchestrated from skyscraper to surface to subway train, experienced by elevator, escalator, windscreen, and aeroplane window.

Corbusier and Pierre Jeanneret collaged Ville Contemporaine into Paris, crudely, in their 'Plan Voisin' (also unbuilt), 1925, a proposal to replace certain so-called 'insalubrious' districts (Figure 14). Presented in striking drawings and models—sponsored by Avions Voisin, makers of luxury cars, and intended to capture politicians' and industrialists' imaginations—the proposal was exhibited at Paris's Exhibition of Decorative Arts in a mock-up of a 'dwelling type' from one of the city blocks. It indicated once again a grid of mass-produced towers which, in an apparent act of social cleansing, were reserved for a 'white-collar' bureaucratic and cultural elite, with labourers and factories nowhere to be seen. Developing Ville Contemporaine, Plan Voisin proposed a rational, scientific, secular city whose centralized planning would tame uncontrolled market-led sprawl—promoting values often

14. Plan Voisin, unbuilt project, 1925. A vision of the ideal city, applied to so-called 'insalubrious' districts of Paris. Housing was concentrated into towers to free up land in between for parks, celebrating the health-giving potential of sunlight and fresh air, in contrast to 19th-century density and pollution. A grid of highways sought to plan in modern infrastructures, rather than retrofit them piecemeal. (Architect: Le Corbusier.)

associated with socialism and communism. But Corbusier and Jeanneret saw no contradiction in claiming the project's urban form and factory-made housing blocks instead as symbols of the new capitalist order of Fordist mass production.

Ten years later, in 1935, Corbusier updated his urban ideas in the book *Radiant City*. In 1928, he had co-founded a group called the International Congress of Modern Architecture (CIAM: Congrès Internationaux d'Architecture Moderne), which included Gropius, Meyer, Mies, and Rietveld. The group held its fourth meeting on a liner cruising from Marseilles to Athens, where they agreed principles for 'the functional city'. Corbusier wrote up these principles as the so-called 'Athens Charter' to suit his own ends.

It repeated familiar tropes: densifying accommodation into slabs around green space; liberating the ground from traffic for parkland; and separating out uses (like housing from industry and transport). In *Radiant City*, however, Corbusier added an extendable grid plan, organizing the city's functions according to the metaphor of a human body. The business and administrative centre would be placed at the top of the plan as the 'head' of Radiant City. Residential areas below would form the 'lungs', set out in grid squares separated by major highways, with housing blocks enclosing giant courtyards and gardens. The cultural centre comprised the 'heart', beneath which was heavy industry, the 'feet'. This time, everyone—workers and managers—shared similar housing as part of an egalitarian technocratic society supposedly balancing urban and rural, work and family, capitalism and centralized planning.

The closest that Radiant City came to realization was at the new city of Chandigarh in India. When India and Pakistan were partitioned after independence in 1947, so was the state of Punjab. Its capital, Lahore, was allocated to Pakistan, and Indian Punjab decided to build a new capital. Corbusier was appointed masterplanner after the original American architect died in 1951, and his designs for Chandigarh followed Radiant City principles. Its Parliament, High Court, and Secretariat buildings (also designed by Corbusier) are at the head, with various grid-plan 'sectors' below containing housing, culture, commerce, and industry, separated by highways. It may have been counter-intuitive at that time to design a car-oriented city for a population then with few cars, and to appoint a Western architect for a postcolonial capital, but Chandigarh has now become a highly liveable city.

The ideals of Ville Contemporaine—planning cities around infrastructure with access for all to hygiene and green space; concentrating urban life into dense blocks; separating uses, and separating pedestrians from traffic; *plus* the underlying conceit that an ideal city could be planned at all—remained largely polemical in the early 20th century. Garden City, Radiant City, and their counterparts were provocations: *against* slums, unplanned sprawl, deprivation, and insanitary conditions; *for* the potential of modern technology, and planned infrastructure, to alleviate urban problems. In postwar times, however, after the extensive destruction of European, Soviet, and Asian cities, Corbusier's provocations started to look plausibly buildable, inspiring numerous postwar reconstructions. Corbusier never took Plan Voisin as seriously in 1925 as certain Western and Soviet planners did after 1945. Some of them actually *did* collage likenesses of Ville Contemporaine into the remains of historic cities. And they frequently did it too quickly and cheaply. The results were widely vilified. Indeed, disorder, density, and the restriction of planning—condemned in the early 20th century—became reappraised in the early 21st as symbolizing urban spontaneity, vigour, and human freedom.

Brutal images

The significant artistic and cultural outpouring following the First World War was decisive in the emergence of modern architecture, including the early projects of Gray, Rietveld, Mies, and Corbusier. But the aftermath of the Second World War was different. Widespread destruction—and stark memories of genocide—meant that the project of rebuilding seemed more raw in 1945 than it had in 1918. In places most affected, there was less desire to rethink, more an impetus simply to put life back together and forge a new normal. In urban design, this involved reaching for interwar templates that held promise. These included the idea of town planning and, sometimes, the formula of Ville Contemporaine. It also involved the widespread adoption of modern architecture. The rise of conflict—particularly the rise of fascism—emerged, at least partly, out of ordinary people's disaffection with elites. Authorities wanted to highlight that the postwar world could be different, that renewed communities could be built out of the ashes. And prewar experiments in modern architecture were already there, ripe for reconstruction, as readymade symbols of the new. Reinforced concrete—open to resculpting, always ambiguous enough to have new meanings projected onto it—became an important medium for refreshed architectural experiment.

Corbusier's architecture caught the imagination of critics once more in the postwar years, despite his ambiguous wartime record (which involved collaborating with the Nazi-sympathizing regime of Vichy France and also being rejected by it). The reinvention of both his work and modern architecture became symbolized by his studio's so-called Unité d'Habitation in Marseille—an untranslatable name, something like Unitary Living Block—commissioned as a government prototype in late 1945 and inaugurated in 1952 (Figure 15).

The Marseille Unité was imagined as a fragment of Radiant City: a neighbourhood for 1,600 people in one sixteen-storey slab. It largely contained flats, which were slotted together in an ingenious interlocking section. One floor of each flat ran the full width of the building, permitting cross-ventilation in summer, with an additional half-floor opening-up a double-height living space. Internal corridors on every third level provided access, supervised by kitchen windows, with parcel lockers for each flat and hatches for delivering communally manufactured ice (preceding the widespread use of fridges). The flats' living spaces opened onto balconies that doubled as shading devices, named *brises soleil*. Corbusier's collaborator Charlotte Perriand detailed bespoke fittings including kitchen units and polished timber handles. A glazed 'street' on the seventh floor hosted community shops, including a convenience store, newsagent, and hairdresser. A rooftop school opened onto a recreation deck containing a pool and exercise facilities. A concierge supervised the entrance, and lift attendants were proposed.

15. Unité d'Habitation, Marseilles, France, 1952. A neighbourhood for 1,600 people in one sixteen-storey slab, with flats slotted together in an ingenious interlocking section, and a glazed 'street' on the seventh-floor hosting community shops. Living spaces opened onto balconies which doubled as shading devices. A rooftop school addressed a recreation deck containing a pool and exercise facilities. The rough concrete—named 'béton brut'—became an inspiration for so-called 'brutalism'. (Architect: Le Corbusier.)

While Corbusier primarily imagined the Unité as an idea about community, architectural critics focused instead on its appearance, shocked by its rough concrete finishes. No attempt was made to hide the grain traced by individual boards of the concrete formwork, to reduce the number of so-called 'blow holes' pockmarking the surface, to polish-out marks where wet concrete slopped around the top of each 'lift' of formwork, or to repair imperfections. Corbusier argued these decisions were economic—disingenuously, given that he was allowed to exceed standard state budgets—and reflected human characteristics:

The defects shout at one from all parts of the structure! Luckily, we have no money!…Exposed concrete shows…incidents of the shuttering, the joints of the planks, the fibres and knots of the wood. [In] men and women do you not see the wrinkles and birthmarks, the crooked noses…?

The commission was a sop to Corbusier when the French government was awarding big projects, including the rebuilding of war-damaged towns like St Dié and Le Havre, to other architects. The latter went to Auguste Perret, for whom Corbusier had worked in the 1920s and who sought to refine concrete surfaces as 'poured stone' in the tradition of Hennebique. The Unité rejected Perret's perfectionist values, and Corbusier instead revelled deliberately in crude, gloopy concrete—named *béton brut* in French—claiming he was elevating economic necessity into a symbol of the age.

Critics were also exercised by the Marseille Unité's sculptural imagery. Gone were the delicate *piloti* of modernism's early 'uniform', pumped up instead as massive splayed legs. Gone were the sheer white planes with thin sills and drips, flattening elevations in an illusion of machine production, replaced with deep *brises soleil* in primary colours. Gone was the curved plane of Villa Savoye's sundeck, superseded by a roofscape of enigmatic concrete objects: funnels, a shell vault, blocks, and steps. The Unité illustrated a renewed concern for form, texture, and colour, echoing the swelling shapes of Corbusier's latest artworks inspired by full-bodied naked figures, and the so-called 'primitive' art of folk cultures. Architects who subscribed to the 'teenage uniform' became troubled by what they saw as the Unité's gratuitous 'formalism', and the ambiguity of its shapes.

Those shapes pursued what we would now call 'intertextuality'. They played games with visual clues, hinting at forms—artistic, natural, and industrial—which themselves hinted at other forms.

The Unité's imagery shared visual sources with interwar modernism, like factories, trains, and boats. But there was also another layer of subtler, stranger visual codes at work which were altogether harder to place. These included echoes of prehistoric sculptures and paintings—imagined as being timeless and before style, and associated with classlessness—acknowledging the war's disruption of traditional hierarchies and cultural codes. They also included references to wartime concrete bunkers and bomb shelters, and to Picasso's painting and sculpture (the artist spent a day with Corbusier discussing the Marseille drawings). The Unité illustrated the idea that altered images of modernity seemed necessary to express a revised postwar understanding of society and technology. Following mechanized warfare, incendiary bombs—and especially the Nazi Holocaust and atomic bombs dropped on Hiroshima and Nagasaki, 1945—technology no longer seemed such an innocent emblem of progress. Numerous modern architects with little opportunity to build in wartime, or rejected by fascist regimes that favoured romanticized nationalistic imagery, had spent time strategizing for postwar reconstruction at all scales: from Corbusier's ideal cities to Jane Drew's designs for ideal kitchens. And, for Corbusier, the Unité's *béton brut*, *brises soleil*, sculptural forms, and vivid colours fulfilled the promise of such strategies, yielding a revised imagery for postwar modern architecture, proposing a kind of technological prehistory.

Intertextual imagery also characterized the other most striking postwar Corbusier project: the Chapel of Notre Dame du Haut, Ronchamp, 1949, on a hilltop surveying the Vosges mountains, replacing a chapel destroyed in war. Corbusier, with Protestant ancestry and rakish tastes, was an odd appointment for the Catholic establishment, but he was championed by Dominican monk Father Couturier who edited the magazine *Sacred Art*.

The chapel seemed radically new but also strangely familiar (Figure 16). A weighty, swelling roof over-sailed the chapel's massively thick south wall, punctured with numerous deep

16. Chapel of Notre Dame du Haut, Ronchamp, France, 1949.
Radically new and yet strangely familiar, three towers project above
a swelling roof which over-sails the chapel's massive south wall,
punctured with deep windows of apparently random size and
placement. The curving east elevation contains an outdoor altar
and pulpit with an icon of the Virgin Mary skewered on a rod in a
window above. The chapel works on the levels of raw experience and
academic sophistication, ambiguous enough to keep offering fresh
meanings. (Architect: Le Corbusier.)

windows of apparently random size and placement. It also
over-sailed the concave east elevation, containing an outdoor
altar and pulpit, with an icon of the Virgin Mary skewered on a
rod in a window above. Three curved towers, two back-to-back
and one at right angles, loomed over the roof, which sloped to
a giant spout washing rainwater into a pool containing a concrete
pyramid and cone. The cave-like interior, whose floor inclined
with the hillside, was reached through an outsize pivoting
door enamelled with a bright allegorical mural. The placement
of key interior elements—altar, cross, pulpit, pews—reflected the
geometry of the bulging ceiling. And the darkness within was
punctured by shafts of illumination from the various openings,

supplemented by ethereal light emanating from a thin strip of perimeter glass where the roof was lifted slightly above the walls.

The chapel was engineered to achieve the forms Corbusier wanted, rather than following the logic of its materials. Its seemingly weighty roof was actually constructed like an aeroplane wing from slender struts. The walls were not solid concrete, as they first appear, but instead concrete frame infilled with rubble from the previous chapel, or reinforcement mesh onto which cement was sprayed, all covered over with white render.

The chapel pursued Corbusier's enigmatic ideas about order and balance. Charles Jencks likened its shape to 'a nun's cowl, a monk's hood, a ship's prow, praying hands...[all] suggested...and denied at the same time'. Its towers have been imagined as standing stones, Neolithic funerary monuments, and vessels. Its forms have been read in the erotic terms of the naked body, as bellies, buttocks and breasts, and its sprayed concrete as human skin. The multiple meanings of its shapes echo Corbusier's paintings, made concrete in search of poetic potential for postwar modern architecture. To his champions, the chapel represented a profoundly evocative rumination on human spirituality, its strange forms articulating enigmatically the ineffable mysteries of existence.

As with other kinds of intertextuality in film and literature, the more you know—in this instance about art, architecture, theology, and philosophy—the more the chapel gives back. This is not to say that 'clever' readings are right and 'unknowing' readings are wrong. Rather, it works on the levels of both raw experience and academic sophistication, done with sufficient ambiguity to keep offering fresh interpretations.

Like the Unité, the chapel again broke the tentative conventions of modern architecture. British architect James Stirling suggested that it prompted a 'crisis of rationalism', its striking 'plastic' forms requiring committed modernists to revisit the principles of their work. Ronchamp and the Unité took concrete from a straightforward expression of modernity—replacing loadbearing walls with frames and planes—to something altogether more complex, simultaneously modern and prehistoric. Both buildings spawned imitations, from close copies to comparable intertextual exercises.

Corbusier built five more Unités in France and Germany, but it was the Marseille block that became the model for swathes of Cold War housing in both the free-market West and communist East. Despite being widely copied, it was rarely understood well by its imitators. Raw concrete, which fared adequately in Marseille's hot dry climate, survived less well in climates with damaging cycles of freeze and thaw. The Unité's community facilities—shops, recreation roofscape, concierge, and lift attendants—rarely figured in the copies, producing housing silos that were often isolating, failing to mitigate anti-social behaviour. The Unité model thus became condemned as a failure.

In postwar decades, *béton brut*, and the intertextual form-making associated with it, symbolized a decisive rejection of the terror wrought by fascism. It described a new beginning—imagined partly in relation to ancient beginnings—which aspired to recombine community, technology, and architecture with a renewed sense of purpose. Today, however, that aspiration has been largely forgotten. *Béton brut* got tainted by the reputation of failed high-rise housing. And that failure continues to colour how people think about concrete architecture, and—indeed—modern architecture altogether.

Global brutalisms

Using the term 'brutalism' to celebrate the architecture of *béton brut* must rate as one of the worst promotional ideas ever. Banham popularized the term in his 1966 book *The New Brutalism: Ethic or Aesthetic?* It emerged from young British architects' reactions against postwar housebuilding there, where cheap modern-ish picturesque cottages became branded 'the new humanism'. Banham's book collected the work of young architects who found this bland and who, inspired by the imagery of the Unité and Ronchamp, parodied it with a Corbusian 'new brutalism'. Banham's subtitle illustrated how Brutalists believed their architecture had both a distinctive look and a moral purpose, adding expressive materials and bold shapes to the interwar modern imagery of function and structure. Brutalism meant dramatic silhouettes, the clear display of structure, 'primitive' traditions in art, celebrating the 'essences' of materials in their raw 'as-found' state—not only, but importantly, reinforced concrete—and the nickname, 'Brutus', of one of Banham's friends: the male half of architect duo Alison and Peter Smithson. The Smithsons' own evolving definition focused more on Brutalism's 'ethic', emphasizing concerns with people's everyday lives.

When Brutalism fell out of favour, the name allowed its detractors to dismiss its buildings as brutal in their treatment of people. That's how Brutalism is popularly remembered, forgetting how the term once declared ambitions for postwar rebuilding. Indeed, modern architecture's detractors have since expanded the term beyond what was recognized as Brutalism at the time to dismiss pretty much any modern building they don't like.

Banham's British examples of Brutalism came from the offices of the Smithsons, Stirling and Gowan, Denys Lasdun, and Ernö Goldfinger, adding examples from Western Europe, Japan, and the Americas. The term caught on, also employed to describe buildings from the offices of Paul Rudolph and Louis I. Kahn in the USA, and notably Kallmann, McKinnell, and Knowle's striking Boston City Hall. Indeed, Brutalism became more international than the International Style ever was, although influential Western critics struggled to acknowledge its global diversity.

Brazil's modern architecture *did* get noticed in the West following a MoMA exhibition in 1943 which simultaneously celebrated and patronized Brazilian architectural culture. The 1936 Ministry of Health building in Rio de Janeiro, designed by Lucio Costa and his team, anticipated the Marseille Unité by nine years: clad in *brises soleil*, with a sculptural roofscape. Not yet quite Brutalist, it nevertheless looked substantially weightier than regular interwar modernism. Western histories say this building quotes from Corbusier's work, acknowledging time Corbusier spent in Rio, failing to recognize that the trade in ideas was clearly mutual. Costa's projects of the 1930s and 1940s combined *brises-soleil*, verandahs, and trellises with local elements—artisan tilework, tiled panels, and Portugese mosaics—and he argued (as Elisabetta Andreoli and Adrian Forty note) that it was these 'local elements which made Brazilian architecture "modern"'. Brazilian Brutalists produced remarkable work, among them João Batista Vilanova Artigas, Paolo Mendes de Rocha, Jorge Machado Moriera, Fabio Penteado, and Oscar Niemeyer. Niemeyer became most famous. His Church of St Francis in Pampulha, Belo Horizonte, 1940—a group of timber-lined, mosaic-finished, concrete shell vaults, connected to a chimney-like 'campanile' by a tilted canopy—was so radical that the Church initially refused to consecrate it.

Costa masterplanned Brazil's new capital, Brasília—begun 1956, inaugurated 1960, and designated a World Heritage Site in 1987. Its sleek government buildings, from Niemeyer's studio, strike dramatic poses against a flat horizon. The thin twin concrete towers of the National Congress, 1960, sit across a podium from the Senate—a dome—and the Chamber of Deputies—a matching inverted dome—both 1958.

Italian-born Brazilian architect Lina Bo Bardi only became famous posthumously. The structure of her São Paulo Museum of Art, 1968—a concrete 'portico' standing only on two pairs of legs placed a huge 70 metres apart—created a public plaza at ground level, opening views from Trianon Park to the city (Figure 17).

17. São Paulo Museum of Art, São Paulo, Brazil, 1968. A dramatic illustration of the power of so-called 'brutalist' imagery. A concrete 'portico', standing on only two pairs of legs placed a huge 70 metres apart, makes a public plaza at ground level, opening views from Trianon Park to the city. (Architect: Lina Bo Bardi.)

Andreoli and Forty argue that newness is particularly valued in Brazil, where little architecture isn't either new or decayed. Famous Brutalist buildings there, they suggest, remain more current than buildings finished since.

If Western critics patronized Brazilian brutalism, they mostly ignored the Soviet Union—partly because it was harder to find information in the Cold War, but largely because they barely tried—and Soviet architects were always more conversant with Western ideas. Western critics stereotyped Soviet modernism as blank and rigidly functional, characterized by prefabricated concrete slab blocks and windswept plazas. Indeed, that perception prevails today, ignoring some striking projects and innovations. The Soviet bloc was a centralized economy where the general secretary of the Communist Party dictated architectural policy. Nikita Krushchev, who governed from 1953 to 1964, rejected Stalin's decorative preferences and, seeking to solve a massive housing crisis, championed prefabrication, directing that 90 per cent of buildings should be built using prefabricated concrete panel systems. Numerous iterations, technical developments, profiles, and textures of these systems proved innovative and effective. But the non-system built projects, mostly cultural and government institutions, now attract most attention. Leonid Brezhnev, general secretary from 1964 to 1982, encouraged more architectural freedom. The resulting diversity of invention has sometimes been included in the category of Brutalism, for example: a stack of double storey Jenga blocks containing offices for the Georgian Ministry of Highways in Tibilisi, 1974, designed by G. Tschachawa and colleagues; cantilevered swooping twin cinemas at Rossiya, Yerevan, Armenia, designed by A. Tarkhanyan and colleagues in 1975; and a faceted ovaloid hotel perched above a beach on three giant circular legs, designed by Igor Vailevsky, in Yalta, Ukraine, 1985. Western publishers have recently discovered these projects, albeit depicting them as kitschy communist chic while scarcely acknowledging their spatial and formal innovations.

Almost two-thirds of African nations were liberated from Western colonizers between 1957 and 1966. Brutalism and *béton brut* frequently provided architectural symbols of independence, representing new nations forged in a modern technological world. The resulting buildings could be somewhat contradictory, however. The domed National Museum of Ghana in Accra, 1957, curated an idea of Ghanaian national identity following the 19th-century Western model of the national museum, and its architects—Maxwell Fry, Jane Drew, Lindsay Drake, and Denys Lasdun—were hired from Britain, the former colonizer. Economic development in postcolonial Africa sometimes emphasized the sale of minerals and extraction rights, frequently involving Western-owned international corporations, who have been seen as colonizers of another kind. Indeed, the idea of the architect as professional consultant, and the idea that architecture should symbolize modernity, were also Western imports. Israeli architects were sometimes hired for nation-building projects in African countries to address the contradictions. From another former colony—one which forged a reputation for modern architecture as Mandatory Palestine in the interwar period—they seemed sympathetic to the issues. Examples include Hôtel Ivoire in Abidjan, Ivory Coast, 1970, designed by Thomas Leitersdorf and Heinz Fenchel, and Ife University in Nigeria, 1972, designed by Areih Sharon. The striking Findeco House in Lusaka, Zambia, 1976, designed by Yugoslav architects Dušan Milenkovic and Branimir Ganovic, illustrates how architects were also hired in some new African nations from Soviet Eastern Europe.

Specific national and regional modern architectures, and prominent African architects, frequently emerged only some years after liberation. In Senegal, for example, the Brutalism of Pierre Goudiaby Atepa—like the Atepa Group Headquarters, 1977—and Cheikh N'Gom—including Immeuble Fayçal, Dakar, 1984—was marked by sculptural forms characterized by distinctive pyramidal shapes.

Until the 21st century, the global architectural media tended only to recognize buildings in Africa designed by European and American architects, plus those that conformed to Western expectations. And such projects were frequently written up as a generic 'tropical architecture', rather than as specific buildings for specific sites in specific cultures.

Banham's term *New Brutalism* stuck, albeit at the lasting expense of its architecture. In some Western cultures, like the UK, property developers have recently exploited the poor cultural reputation of Brutalism to demolish and densify valuable sites for substantial profit. In such instances, it became expedient to assume that all concrete architecture was Brutalist, and all Brutalist architecture was undesirable. Meanwhile, in various global cultures—like Brazil, and certain postcolonial African countries—Brutalist buildings maintain different associations, frequently marking positive change and freedom from colonial repression.

Metabolists, megastructures, and mats

If Radiant City represented the translation of interwar modernism into urban form, then the 'megastructure' came to represent Brutalist urban form. The term was popularized by Banham (again), but first coined in Japan by architect Fumihiko Maki, who was part of the so-called 'metabolism group', including Kenzō Tange. Tange's office famously designed a peace memorial and exhibition hall at Hiroshima, 1955, claimed for Brutalism. Simultaneously, Tange was conducting academic research with colleagues at the University of Tokyo's Urban Lab, investigating the densification of that city in response to a perceived lack of building sites there. Statistical modelling was used to analyse commuting patterns, transport, and traffic congestion, testing migration theory in relation to economic development.

This work tapped broader contemporary intellectual currents around so-called 'systems thinking'. Systems thinking understood everything—from aeroplanes to traffic flows to human bodies and natural landscapes—as complex, interrelated systems that could be measured and analysed mathematically. Motivated by the earliest computers fed with punch cards, it prompted its followers to think systematically—like computers—encouraging the extensive analysis of data and imagining issues like urban sprawl as problems to be solved. This approach tapped into a renewed technological optimism in the late 1950s and early 1960s. Prompted by early televisions and fridges installed in prosperous homes, by the Soviets' first satellite, Sputnik, by NASA's moonshots and burgeoning air travel, systems thinking appeared to propose the scientific transformation of everyday life in Western cultures.

'Metabolist' architects—including Tange, Kiyonoru Kikutake, and Kisho Kurokawa—made two key arguments. First, that different parts of the city—like urban core and suburb—have different rates of 'metabolic' change. Second, that new land needed in Tokyo and other cities could be made by reclaiming the sea, and decking-over infrastructure like railways, motorways, and even existing districts. Megastructures were conceived as built land: fixed infrastructures, sometimes kilometres long, enabling development. They were imagined as technical frameworks, planned according to social theories, for systematizing transport and service provision.

Tange proposed several unbuilt megastructures. The Boston Harbour Development Project, designed with MIT students in 1959, proposed giant A-frame containers, with motorways and transit systems at their base, into which buildings could be slotted. The striking images and models elevated *béton brut* to another level of monumentality. The Tokyo Bay Project, 1960, proposed an 18-kilometre concrete framework across the water comprising two parallel motorways whose loops made sub-districts, with offshoots leading to housing sectors (Figure 18). Its open-ended structure allowed whole districts of buildings to be infilled, imagined as capable of unlimited extension.

In 1963, Georges Candilis, Alexis Josic, and Shadrach Woods, with Manfred Schiedhelm won a competition to design a building for the new Free University in West Berlin. Like Tange's megastructures, it was designed for infinite extension and perpetual change. The architects conceived groups of rooms as clusters within a larger structure, divided by corridors imagined as a grid of alleyways and courtyards like an Arabic medina. The interior was a kind of labyrinth. Entrances around the building's perimeter were deliberately multiplied to contradict the hierarchies of conventional universities, with their grand entrances and marble halls, conceiving the building instead as a city district. The concrete-framed structure was finished with a pattern of windows and 'cor-ten' (rusty) steel panels that, in theory at least, could be reconfigured to suit internal alterations. Alison Smithson

18. Tokyo Bay megastructure, unbuilt project, 1960. Another ideal city proposal: a dramatic concrete framework comprising two parallel motorways whose loops made sub-districts, with offshoots leading to housing sectors. It illustrated so-called 'systems thinking': an open-ended structure allowing districts of buildings to be infilled, imagined as capable of unlimited extension. (Architect: Kenzō Tange.)

referred to mini-megastructures like the Free University—and Corbusier's contemporaneous project for a Venice hospital—as 'mat buildings', thinking their plans looked like Turkish rugs. She argued that they comprised a system of basic units—streets, rooms, and squares—repeated and varied like a child's puzzle.

Dutch architect John Habraken claimed the megastructure was a political idea. His book *Supports: An Alternative to Mass Housing*, 1961, argued that the state should provide infrastructure for housing—the 'supports'—and that people should construct buildings themselves within those supports. He promoted 'self-build': empowering people to construct their own homes. The image of Habraken's megastructures diverged from Tange's

Brutalist consistency. They were characterized instead as a chaotic, spontaneous assembly of homes expressing individual character. Habraken's vision remained contradictory, simultaneously bottom-up and top-down, celebrating both centralized control *and* the power of individual choice.

The most striking built megastructure was a housing cooperative named 'Habitat' in Montreal, Canada, made for the 1967 Expo there (Figure 19). Designed by Moshie Safdie, it comprised 354 standardized rectangular modules. Constructed by stacking prefabricated concrete boxes like Lego bricks, it drew its imagery from traditional Mediterranean villages and Italian hill towns. Its stepping form looked impossibly complicated but was guided by a systematic order of structure and repetition.

19. Habitat, Montreal, 1967. A model community whose imagery drew from traditional Mediterranean villages and hill towns. Constructed by stacking prefabricated concrete boxes, its stepping form looked impossibly complicated but was guided by a rigorous order of structure and repetition. (Architect: Moshe Safdie.)

Habitat was directly descended from Hennebique's house, its pattern of terraces extending the logic of the cantilever and the roof garden, taking the imagery of concrete modern architecture to a further extreme. However, if steel was readily imagined as a kit of parts, then the architectural and urban logics of reinforced concrete always remained more ambiguous. Concrete could make frames, planes, cantilevers, and sculptural shapes, be extended into megastructures, structure communities, and be formed with a profound sense of human purpose. It could constitute the sleek surfaces of the five points or be roughed-up as *béton brut*. The modernity of its imagery stemmed primarily from its potential to assume novel forms, and its capacity to portray intertextual references. Somehow, reinforced concrete architecture could stand for industry and domesticity, capitalism and socialism, planning and spontaneity, the sacred and the profane, newness and ancientness all at once. More than steel, concrete always illustrated modernity's double edged-ness, recalling both the social opportunities of technology and the continuing unease surrounding technology's consequences. When Corbusier and others wrestled with concrete's material complexities, they found they were wrestling directly with the cultural complexities of modernity itself. Ultimately, concrete finishes became only patchily accepted. And 'brutal' and 'ugly' became lazy ciphers for their multiple ambiguities. Concrete encouraged the re-imagination of modern architecture, but its peculiarities also exposed modern architecture to question. That remained both its strength and its weakness.

Chapter 4
Brick

Another tradition of modern architecture

Few cowsheds figure in the histories of architecture. One that does, along with an adjacent barn, was completed in 1925 on Gut Gurkau Farm near Lübeck, Germany, to designs by Hugo Häring (Figure 20). Häring was part of a group called 'The Ring', which included Mies, that rejected architectural decoration in favour of technical efficiency. The cowshed's farmer client believed agriculture should be rethought rationally, and Häring justified his designs functionally, developing them in relation to technical research. He noted proudly that 'the disposal of dung from the stalls is achieved in a single channel without reversal', adding that, because of the curving plan, 'the animals do not stand directly opposite each other, so the threat of infection through inhaling one another's contaminated breath is reduced'. The adjacent barn had a remarkable 'lamella' roof—an outsize upside-down boat—replacing traditional rafters with a 'gridshell' of criss-crossed timbers. This too was justified functionally, because it improved structural efficiency, and reduced the sizes of timbers required.

Freed from the complex cultural associations of buildings for humans, the cowshed became interpreted as an ideal translation of a sequence of tasks into a building, as a leading example of

20. Cowshed at Gut Garkau Farm, Germany, 1925. Initially interpreted as an ideal translation of a sequence of tasks into a building—a leading example of 'functionalism'—it later became reappraised for its bold imagery, and then as a symbol of a less rigid modern architecture accepting modernity as an extension of history, rather than a rejection of it. (Architect: Hugo Häring.)

functionalism. Likewise, the barn roof was understood as a novel but straightforward expression of function. Häring's functionalist buildings looked different to those of Mies and Gropius, however—being shapelier, curving in plan and section—and because, while their forms were clearly new, they were constructed in traditional materials of brick, timber, and tile.

Brutalists in the 1960s reappraised these farm buildings, celebrating their bold imagery more than the functionalist arguments. Other critics reappraised them again in the 1970s and 1980s, claiming them instead as symbols of a lost path in modern architecture. These critics—including Christian Norberg-Schulz, Kenneth Frampton, Peter Blundell Jones, and Colin St John

Wilson, architect of the British Library—championed the idea of 'another tradition' of modern architecture, arguing that a wrong turn was taken in the 1920s and 1930s. They continued to celebrate modern architecture as a reflection of up-to-date culture, novel construction, new forms of social life, and changed imagery. But they suggested that it lost its way in the interwar years. Ideas about zoning cities became too rigid, they believed, the organization of buildings around functions became too hard-line, and the categories of the International Style and the five points became too formulaic. Historians have suggested that these criticisms crystallized during postwar meetings of CIAM, when a group of 'angry young men'—including Alison (!) and Peter Smithson, Aldo van Eyck, Georges Candilis, and Shadrach Woods—challenged the orthodoxies of prewar modernism and the urban forms of the Athens Charter. These differences came to a head at CIAM's tenth meeting in Dubrovnik, 1956, where this group organized an informal breakaway named Team 10. When CIAM voted itself out of existence in 1959, Team 10 continued to meet. The group is now credited with more influence than it had at the time, largely because the divergent stories of its protagonists have helped historians illustrate the increasing diversity of postwar modern architecture.

Alison Smithson, the group's self-appointed historian, collected their ideas and projects from the 1950s and 1960s in her *Team 10 Primer*. She argued that the group was less concerned with the image-making of high architecture than with ordinary people's lives in ordinary homes and streets, studying how communities associated with their surroundings, and so-called socio-psychological needs. Key reference points were academic anthropologists: 'structuralists', who looked for patterns in people's inhabitation of their surroundings across different times and cultures. Many Team 10 members acknowledged globalized trade and capital as inevitable, but also sought to reconnect modern architecture with local cultures and diverse building practices. They preferred to think of architecture's settings in terms of 'place'—as the everyday situations and events of human life—rather than 'space'—as an abstract idea. 'Whatever space and time mean,' Aldo van Eyck wrote, 'place and occasion mean more'. Projects by Team 10 architects—such as Ralph Erskine's housing designs in Sweden, and Giancarlo de Carlo's university community perched on a hillside above Urbino, Italy—got included in the catalogues of the 'other tradition'. Like Gut Garkau's barn, they seemed tailored to rhythms of life, and ideas about the sociability of community. This thinking also became associated with the long history of brick as a material. Brick, in the work of architects like Team 10, denoted that modernity might be understood less as a new beginning for human history than as an extension of it.

Many global cultures have traditions of clay or mud brick construction. Evidence exists of the use of fired brick as long ago as 5000 BCE in Mesopotamia, and of decorative brickwork in Babylon in approximately 2300 BCE. In Ancient Rome, fired clay bricks were first used for strengthening the corners of buildings and openings in walls, then for whole buildings from the Age of Augustus (63 BCE–14 CE). The use of cement paste mortars to bind bricks together has been traced to 500 BCE in Ancient Greece, although modern mortars—mixed with Portland Cement—became widespread only in mid-19th-century Europe.

Until the 19th century, brickmaking in northern Europe was largely seasonal. Farmers shaped clay bricks in wooden moulds when there was little other work in winter. The firing of those bricks, requiring temperatures between 900 °C and 1,100 °C, involved as much luck as judgement. Each brick's hardness depended on its proximity to the flames and the heat of the fire. The hardest, most burnt, bricks were waterproof, called 'foundation', 'cellar', or 'arch' bricks, reflecting where they were used. The least baked 'salmon' bricks were soft, set aside for internal partitions. And regular baked bricks, 'commons', were employed for external walls.

These basic brick types persisted after production was industrialized in the mid-19th century. Steam-powered manufacturing, particularly in the USA, added so-called 'wire cut' bricks—trimmed from clay extruded by machines—and sharp-edged 'dry press' bricks—made from clay forced into moulds at high pressure. The most important industrial innovations, however, were in brick firing. Early kilns were made and broken for each firing, but the first permanent Hoffman kiln was constructed in Germany in 1858 with multiple chambers and air ducts to control temperatures accurately. Reliable firing improved the predictability of brickmaking, and increased the range of hardnesses available. At the same time, modern excavation techniques yielded a greater variety of clays in different colours and textures. This extended the possibilities available to architects for expressing brick surfaces, supplementing variety in the 'pointing' of mortar joints (e.g. mortar smeared flush with the bricks, or raked out to create shadows, or expressed as broad or fine lines).

Brick became so important to the advocates of 'another tradition' in modern architecture that their alternative history became more-or-less a collection of famous brick buildings from the period of modernity. That history tended to start with 19th-century Arts and Crafts architecture in Britain; specifically the Red House, Bexleyheath, 1859, designed by Philip Webb for writer, artist, and industrialist William Morris, sometimes promoted as a progenitor of the modern free plan. It emphasized Frank Lloyd Wright's brick houses like the Robie House, 1909, and included the 'expressive' Wright-inspired brickwork of Klint and Klint's Grundtvig Church, Copenhagen, Denmark, 1927, and Willem Dudok's Hilversum Town Hall, the Netherlands, 1931, alongside Häring's cowshed and barn. Their story was that the simplistic visual prescriptions of the International Style overtook modern architecture's original purpose: to rethink architecture for the age of modernity and industrial production. They argued that this alternative lineage—contrasting Gut Garkau with Corbusier's almost contemporary project for a Radiant Farm—showed how modern architecture shouldn't be understood as the refinement of a static set of forms towards perfection, as in Mies's work, but should be understood instead as an ongoing negotiation with diverse localities, peoples, and cultures. It should illustrate a continuing dialogue with ever-changing shifts in modernity, they felt, not be frozen as a static repertoire of forms.

In Chapters 2 and 3, I showed how technical innovations in iron, steel, and reinforced concrete produced new possibilities for organizing architecture and new architectural images, and I highlighted architectural theories emerging in relation to the new imagery. The role of brick in modern architecture was different, however. It was a familiar rather than novel material, and its inherent organizational logic was already well known. The adoption of brick into modern architecture represented instead a challenge to the hard-line view of modernity as a rejection of history, understanding modern architecture differently as a continuation of history.

The local and the national

Critics found a definitive example of this modern brick imagery on the island of Säynätsalo in rural Finland, in a civic building completed in 1951 for a small community centred on a plywood mill, which incorporated a town hall, library, and shops (Figure 21). Its architect, Alvar Aalto, is remembered as the leading light of Scandinavian modern design, combining warm materials with simple shapes to make objects imagined as available to all. Aalto designed mass-produced stools, chairs, light fittings, and glassware in this spirit as well as buildings. His work became characterized as 'expressionist', discussed in terms of 'organic' geometries.

Säynätsalo Town Hall was located on a hillside in a forest clearing. It appeared initially unassuming, arranged around a courtyard with low roofs. The council chamber, rising above the low roof ridges, was expressed as a tower with a distinctive 'butterfly' roof

21. Säynätsalo Town Hall, Finland, 1951. Steps lead from the street to a courtyard surrounded by low roofs, and a council chamber above expressed with a distinctive 'butterfly' roof. The imagery of the complex refers both to modernity and history, to so-called high culture and low culture, recalling the everyday spaces of local farmers and (no less) the Greco-Roman idea of human civilization. (Architect: Alvar Aalto.)

that accentuated its height and emphasized its civic role. The courtyard was wrapped with a glazed cloister, reached by a grand stair leading up from the street. The buildings were constructed from pressed red bricks which Aalto instructed the bricklayers to set slightly out-of-line, giving the walls an undulating rustic quality, playing shadows across their surface in low northern sunlight. The roof of the council chamber, reached by a brick-lined and brick-floored staircase, was supported with timber trusses shaped like upturned hands.

The complex was intense for its diminutive size, accentuated by Aalto-designed fixtures including handles, handrails, and light fittings. Doors were understood not just as openings but as thresholds between realms. Windows were imagined as frames to the forest. Sequences of spaces were conceived as journeys through light and dark, compressing people through smaller spaces and releasing them into larger ones. The experience of the building was carefully choreographed and its details thoughtfully calibrated. Its orderly plan and section were derived from functional needs, and also carefully adapted to local culture, climate, and the topography of the site.

Aalto made plenty of intertextual references. He did this differently to Corbusier, looking more to architectural traditions and the ancient classical past than to industrial forms and artistic shape-making. Säynätsalo Town Hall's organization around a courtyard recalled local farmsteads and the cloisters of historic monasteries. Sat into a slope, it can be read as both a classical temple on a plinth and a fragment of a picturesque Italian hill town. Vertical timber slats fixed to doors and windows hinted at both the fluting of columns in classical architecture and the tree trunks of the surrounding forest. The red brick, here, referred more to humble industrial buildings than grand public ones, and to long traditions of brickmaking. Thus, the building played artful double games. Its imagery combined references to both modernity and history, to so-called high culture and low culture, recalling the everyday spaces of local farmers and (no less!) the Greco-Roman tradition of human civilization. It evoked a northern romance about Mediterranean life, alongside an idea of the forest as psychological retreat that remains prominent in Finnish culture. Critics understood the building as a synthesis of global modernism with local sensibilities, claiming it as an image of modern Finnishness and Scandinavianness.

Identity claims like these relate to a strand of architectural history which seeks national characteristics reflected in buildings, trying to isolate, say, authentically Finnish, or Australian, or Korean architectures. Such histories have usually celebrated premodern buildings—valorizing traditional construction techniques that worked local materials in response to local climates. They tend to identify indigenous characteristics and understand them to be threatened by globalized finance and industry, and by the international industrial building materials which have grown to dominate construction.

Political historian Benedict Anderson argued in his book *Imagined Communities*, 1983, that ideas of nation and nationalism were themselves products of modernity. Anderson linked the modern importance of the nationstate to the overthrow of absolute monarchies in the 18th and 19th centuries in the West. He attributed ideas of the nation to the simultaneous rise of print media and literacy. He connected them to a loss of shared religious values coinciding with the rise of modern science and new economic interests at the time of the Industrial Revolution. It was no coincidence, Anderson argued, that the creation of republics in the Western hemisphere between 1776 and 1838 paralleled the emergence and widespread consumption of national languages, distributed by burgeoning printing presses.

This new notion of nation, associated with ideas of patriotism, took root rapidly. In the 19th century, the construction of museums telling national stories, the first mappings of national territories, and the collection of census data, consolidated formations of nation. Emerging stories about national identities usually included some groups and excluded others, making claims about who belonged and who didn't. Anderson argued that conceptions of nation associated people with others they hadn't yet met by encouraging them to imagine themselves together as a collective. The power of the idea became illustrated by people's willingness to risk their lives for it in war.

Claims about national architectures have always been freighted with difficult questions: what—and therefore who—gets included in, and excluded from, particular national histories; how does architecture get used politically to claim certain ideas of nationhood and reject others? In some postcolonial countries, and in minority nations asserting their identity, the project of cataloguing and producing national architectures has been seen as vital in curating national identity. Examples include the early 20th-century buildings of Antoni Gaudí, linked to Catalan identity, or Oscar Niemeyer's projects symbolizing modern Brazil. Bombastic claims to national architectures have also been made by fascist regimes, who used buildings to aggrandize power and emphasize military might. These included, for example, the puffed-up projects of Albert Speer for Nazi Germany, associated with that regime's sinister nationalist rhetoric of 'blood and soil'. The dark shadows cast by Speer's architecture—and what it stood for—illustrate the risks of any claims to national architectures. Yet, among the champions of the 'other tradition', attempts persisted to claim a role for local identities, cultures, and histories in modernity. They hoped to illustrate that the emergence of global cultures didn't necessarily involve the rejection of local ones. This thinking crystallized in the 1990s around the term 'critical regionalism'—coined by Liane Lefaivre and Alexander Tzonis, and popularized by Kenneth Frampton—which described the idea of indigenous modern architectures sensitive to site, culture, history, and identity. However, champions of critical regionalism have had to work very hard to claim that such architectures—like Säynätsalo Town Hall—are somehow more authentic because they respond to a local sense of place while simultaneously navigating dangerous associations with bombastic nationalisms.

Monumentality and order: Louis I. Kahn

The most striking images of modern brickwork were found in the buildings of Louis I. Kahn (1901–74; no relation to Albert Kahn), the third superhero of modern architecture I'll introduce. If Mies was modernism's obsessive perfectionist, and Corbusier its establishment iconoclast, then Kahn was its zen mystic. Kahn wrote—reminiscent of Taoist philosophy—that a great building 'must begin with the unmeasurable, must go through measurable means when it is being designed, and in the end must be unmeasurable'. Kahn's aura of spirituality was captured in aphorisms like this, which pervaded his accounts of his buildings and his teaching. Like Team 10's members, Kahn emphasized modern architecture's insistence on the expression of structure, material, and function, while also challenging the idea of an International Style as dry and prescriptive. Also like Team 10, Kahn sought to reconnect modern architecture with older ideas about human culture and social life. But, while Team 10 looked to anthropology and 'structuralist' ideas for inspiration, seeking timeless patterns in human behaviour, Kahn looked to architectural history and to mystical ideas about the origins of human imagination. He believed that timeless insights remained present in the mysterious flickers of creative intuition, and in the traces of ancient civilizations found in historic ruins. 'What was has always been,' he wrote, 'what is has always been, and what will be has always been'.

Kahn was born Itze-Leib Schmuilowsky on a Baltic island now called Saaremaa, then in Russia but now in Estonia. His family emigrated to America in 1906—to Philadelphia—changing their names to suit their English-speaking environment. From a poor background, scarred by childhood burns, Kahn was reputedly a shy teenager. But his prodigious talents for drawing and piano playing became noticed. He trained as an architect in his beloved adopted city, at the University of Pennsylvania, whose curriculum was inspired by the classicism of Paris's École des Beaux-Arts. Following a year travelling in Europe in 1928, sketching ancient sites in Italy, Kahn embraced modern architecture. But it was another grand tour—a few months at the American Academy of Rome in 1950/1—that apparently transformed his thinking. Kahn had become prominent in the US architectural profession by the 1950s: a charismatic presence in the T-Square Club for architects in Philadelphia, chair of a Federal Public Housing Agency committee, teaching at Yale University. But it was only in his 50s that Kahn became famous, claiming finally to have found his architectural identity.

The building Kahn credited with this self-discovery was superficially unremarkable: a bath house for the Trenton Jewish Community Center in Ewing Township, New Jersey, 1959, which became a diminutive prototype for subsequent projects (Figure 22). It was designed in collaboration with Anne Tyng, whose deep appreciation of geometry had a decisive influence—although, like many women of modern architecture, her substantial contribution went unrecognized for many years. The plan of the bath house formed a cross comprised of five squares. The central square was an unroofed courtyard, an 'unprogrammed' space initially containing a shallow circular basin. The four surrounding squares were topped with their own sloping 'hipped' roofs. These roofs,

22. Trenton Bath House, Ewing Township, New Jersey, USA, 1959. A simple structure, built from bare blocks with mortar smeared across their surface, topped with cheap felt roof tiles. The original circular basin at the centre of this 'unprogrammed' space was subsequently paved over. The Bath House produced an improbably monumental effect and became the prototype for a series of 'archaic', geometric, monumental buildings designed by Louis I. Kahn's office indebted to architectural history. (Architects: Louis I. Kahn, in collaboration with Anne Tyng.)

with square holes open to the sky at their centres, sat on dumpy square columns containing small spaces. The roofs did not quite touch at the corners, and appeared poised slightly above the columns.

The Trenton bath house seemed humble, built from bare concrete blocks (a sibling of clay brick), with mortar smeared flush with their surface rather than neatly raked out, topped with cheap felt roof tiles. But its effect was improbably monumental. What Kahn meant when he said he'd discovered himself, Neil Levine remarked, is that he'd found a new way to integrate structure and space by reinterpreting architectures of the distant past. The roofs were imagined as the poor but noble cousins of ancient domes. For architects in the know, they referred to the Pantheon in Rome, 126 CE, with its open 'oculus' at the centre. The columns recalled the significance of the column to architecture's classical origins. The result, nevertheless, was inescapably modern. Vincent Scully later claimed an 'archaic force' for Kahn's newly found architecture, arguing that it accepted 'no preconditions, fashions, or habits of design without questioning them profoundly'. The bath house, he believed, rethought architecture from first principles. Levine reflected on its 'abject poverty' and 'the opposition between the archetypal sources of the forms [and] their finish, or lack thereof... that made the structure so provocative'.

Yale University Art Gallery—also designed with Tyng, 1953—developed the approach in a substantial commission. The concrete-framed building had a pared-down plan layout. It appeared superficially Mies-ian, its external walls expressed straightforwardly as planes of brick and glass. Where Mies's college buildings demonstrated an obsession with lightness, however, the Yale gallery revelled in heaviness. It crossed Mies's preference for purity with Corbusier's massive postwar concrete, done more precisely than gloopy *béton brut*. The gallery's floor slabs were over a metre deep, their ceilings expressed as a striking pattern of triangular indentations, or 'coffers'. These 'coffered slabs' made the structure more efficient by using less concrete, and they provided space for building services: the pipes, cables, ducts, stairs, and toilets needed to make the building work. The mass of these ceilings dominated the interiors, producing a weighty sense of calm. Their insistent triangular geometry—matched with one rectangular and one circular stairwell, punched through the floorslabs—tapped the ancient power of primary shapes. The gallery's plan was a geometrical diagram so sophisticated that it came right round again to simplicity. To architects, it demonstrated the pure integration of a building's driving geometric idea with optimized structure and servicing.

The Yale gallery got noticed by the global architectural media. But Kahn's international reputation was consolidated through two laboratory buildings completed in 1965: the Medical Research Towers, later Alfred Newton Richards Building, on the University of Pennsylvania campus; and the Salk Institute, on the edge of the Pacific Ocean at La Jolla in Torrey Pines, California. The Richards Laboratories, constructed in reinforced concrete and clad in brick, proposed an elegant solution to the containment of all the building services needed to make labs work—which became widely copied. Kahn's plans and sections expressed and separated-out 'servant' space (the pipes, cables, ducts, stairs, and toilets) from 'served' space (the laboratories themselves, conceived like artists' studios with panoramic corner windows). The concrete floor was again hollow, so pipes and ducts could run through it. The structure was expressed on the façades with a beam that stepped up between the main vertical columns and the corner, expressing the structural load path in the beam, while serving to enlarge the scientists' corner windows. Kahn imagined this as an elegant fusion of lighting and structural engineering with architectural expression. The underlying diagram of the building, again, was admirably refined.

These ideas were extended at the Salk Institute, famous for its astonishing courtyard—paved starkly in travertine, a stone favoured by the Romans—whose smooth surface was interrupted only by a line of water leading the eye to the ocean horizon beyond. This courtyard's radical simplicity highlighted shadows cast on the surrounding structures by intense Californian sun. Kahn reflected gnomically that 'the sun never knew how great it was until it hit the side of a building'. He felt scientists needed both their labs in 'stainless steel and glass' and separate studies with 'the oak table and rug', expressing these rooms of differing qualities clearly in plan and section. 'The room is the place of the mind,' Kahn ruminated, memorably describing plans like those of the Richards Laboratories and Salk Institute as 'a society of rooms'.

Light and shade in Ahmedabad

Notions about the plan as a society of rooms, about the integration of space, structure, geometry, lighting, and services, about ancient models for institutions, and the dignity of monumental architecture, were summarized in one of Kahn's last projects: the Indian Institute of Management in Ahmedabad, commissioned in 1962, and completed the year Kahn died, 1974 (Figure 23). Kahn collaborated with Indian architect Balkrishna Doshi, who perceived in the American's work a yogic pursuit of ideas about the eternal and the soul. Doshi had suggested Kahn's appointment to the Sarabhai family, who'd already commissioned designs from Corbusier in Ahmedabad. At Doshi's encouragement, Kahn committed to brick as a local material, working with it as the primary structure rather than as a finish to reinforced concrete frames like at Yale and the Richards Labs. It was when Kahn began this project that he famously asked a brick what it wanted to be, projecting the modern idea about seeking logics inherent in novel building materials back onto this traditional material, and pursuing a new imagery for it.

The group of Institute buildings responded to Ahmedabad's tropical climate, to the ancient origins of universities in the architectural form of the monastery, and to the suggestion that

23. Indian Institute of Management, Ahmedabad, India, 1974. An intense conjunction of structure and space, combining material and structural logics, engaging light, shadow, monumentality, and order, fusing pure geometries and ancient architectural images through creative intuition into an architecture that seemed simultaneously new, archaic, and timeless. (Architect: Louis I. Kahn.)

learning happens through human encounters as much as it does through formal teaching. To this end, staff and student dormitories were integrated with the institution; imagined themselves as places of learning. Kahn championed the value of encounter, describing the complex as 'a realm of spaces...connected by ways of walking...high spaces together with low spaces, and various spaces where people can...find the places where they can do what they want to do'.

A shallow entrance ramp and stair, slowing and dignifying arrival, arrived adjacent to the library, envisaged as the symbolic heart of the institute. The teaching building was located in a corner of the plan, its shady cloisters leading past an (unrealized) open amphitheatre to a proposed dining room. Further cloisters, arranged on 45-degree diagonals, led from the tree-shaded plaza at the top of the ramp to rows of dormitories. These were triangular four-storey houses arranged around so-called tea rooms: cool 'unprogrammed' places for impromptu conversations. Each house had twenty individual rooms with linked 'servant' towers containing kitchens and toilets. Further tree-shaded courts were laid out between. The plan was highly ordered but the experience of moving through it was rich and intense, animated by surprising diagonal glimpses and movement between intense sun and deep shade. These sequences echoed Team 10's thinking about maintaining 'labyrinthine clarity' in dense, complex buildings, about the importance of thresholds in enlivening architectural experiences, and exploiting the social potential of 'in-between' spaces. Kahn's sources were largely Western: monastic courtyards, the historic quadrangles of Oxford and Cambridge universities, and dramatic 18th-century etchings of Roman ruins made by Giovanni Battista Piranesi. Nevertheless, as William Curtis has remarked, the building became understood in relation to Indian sources: to the dense urban fabric of Ahmedabad and Jaisalmer, to the linked open spaces of Rajput fortresses, and the spatial sequences of Fatehpur Sikri.

The complex was concerned with light, shadow, and breeze. Kahn imagined that sunlight brought architecture to life, understanding architecture as a canvas for the tracking sun. 'Structure is the maker of light,' he wrote: 'a column and a column brings light between.' It was the prevailing wind direction, though, that drove the 45-degree geometry and the design of cloisters and tea rooms as breeze catchers. Kahn echoed Victor and Aladar Olgyay's 1963 book *Design with Climate*, subtitled *Bioclimatic Approach to Architectural Regionalism*, which discussed the adaptation of modern architecture to local climates. The buildings' various openings were understood, like Corbusier's *brises soleil*, as shadow makers, acknowledging how shade and breeze facilitate sociability, creating places for people to stop and talk.

While Kahn believed that this promotion of social life was central to his designs, it was their imagery that primarily attracted the critics' attention. Kahn was reputedly unhappy with the Miesian elevations of the Yale Art Gallery, expressed as thin planes of brick and glass. He believed he'd brought monumentality to the interiors there but not the façades. The Indian Institute of Management's elevations represented Kahn's solution to this perceived problem: plain brick surfaces with giant geometric perforations—circles, arches, and rectangles. These perforations spanned multiple floors with smaller openings behind, recessed in shadow. Where there were window frames, these were set deep so they disappeared into darkness. Alongside the shading function, this made the brickwork appear monumental, recalling Kahn's favourite Roman ruins. While circles, triangles, and rectangles had become established in Kahn's architectural vocabulary by this time, they also recalled the geometries of the 18th-century Jantar Mantar observatories in Delhi and Jaipur.

The Institute's giant circular openings were understood as an arch sat on top of an inverted arch. The arch represented, to Kahn, what brick wanted to be, demonstrating the structural logic of the material: an inherent illustration of how structural loads get transmitted to the ground through masonry. But, in this earthquake zone, Kahn imagined the circle to be a structural idea just as powerful as the arch. Here, the inverted arch comprising the bottom half of the circle would occasionally be called upon, in a quake, to bear loads in the same way that a conventional arch does in normal conditions. Earthquakes also justified Kahn's inclusion of so-called blind arches (arches infilled with brick) to reinforce and animate some of the walls, and characterful concrete lintels inserted into the base of certain arches to provide extra strength. These lintels were a knowing reference, for architects, to the gateway at the Royal Saltworks at Arc-et-Senans, France, 1776, designed by Claude Nicolas Ledoux. They served to highlight the structural nature of the brick walls, reinforcing brick's material logic by highlighting where brick *wasn't* able to perform as well structurally: in tension, where the base of an arch wants to spread outwards as loads push down on it. The concrete lintels here were the exception that proved the rule for Kahn, highlighting the masonry logic of brickwork.

Kahn's geometric openings, like the Institute as a whole, illustrated his distinctive idea of modern architecture. They represented an intense conjunction of structure and space, combining material and structural logics; engaging light, shadow, monumentality, and order; fusing pure geometries and ancient architectural images through creative intuition into buildings that seemed simultaneously new, archaic, and timeless.

Kahn's buildings became respected for their intellectual integrity but were less copied than those of Mies or Corbusier. American architect Peter Eisenman later argued that Kahn's work sowed the seeds of modern architecture's destruction. Kahn, he claimed melodramatically, 'murdered modern architecture' through his return to monumentality and historic motifs. Whether or not this claim has validity, Kahn's designs reinforced claims to another tradition of modern architecture, in brick, negotiating between the forces of global modernity and the particular sites and social situations of buildings.

Refashioning architecture from first principles

If Kahn's work illustrated how modern architecture could remain a way of thinking rather than a formula, then the Church of St Peter at Klippan, Sweden, 1966, illustrated how idiosyncratic such thinking could be. There's a story about its reclusive architect, Sigurd Lewerentz, standing on site holding a handful of nails contemplatively. Asked what he was going to do with them, he apparently replied 'I don't know yet, but I'm not just going to nail two pieces of wood together.' Every architectural element was rethought at St Peter's, making familiar things strange again. At a time when construction and building components were becoming increasingly industrialized and mass produced,

Lewerentz was on site almost daily, inventing bespoke details with the foreman and bricklayers.

The church seems low on first approach, its horizontal roofline punctured only by a chimney. Visitors navigate almost completely around the building to find the door, their path enclosed by an 'L'-shaped wing containing the parish hall and offices: a laborious entrance sequence reputedly expressing the difficulty of finding God. The interior of the church appears like a dark cave (Figure 24). From inside, its windows seem just holes in the walls: an illusion achieved by omitting window frames altogether and instead fixing glass sheets over the outer face of the wall with bronze clips.

The empty church echoes to the sound of water dripping continuously from the font—a giant sea shell fixed to a metal frame—into a gutter in the floor, apparently recalling life's distant origins in water. Not only were its unadorned walls, undulating floors, and vaulted ceilings made from the same slim brown brick, so were certain seats, tables, and—notably—the altar. This furniture seemingly emitted from the floor, giving the impression that the whole church was carved from a giant block of brickwork. The brick vaulted ceilings were supported by a steel column and beam formed into a 'T'—unmistakeably, if not immediately, recalling the symbol of the cross. Its square plan rejected the traditional 'basilica' church plan (divided into nave, aisles, and sanctuary), recalling instead a myth about the earliest Christian services as a group of worshippers gathered in an arc around a priest.

Bricks are usually laid in a regular pattern called a 'bond'. In accepted bricklaying practice, if you stand beneath a brick wall and look straight up, the vertical edges of the bricks (the 'perpends') should line-up. Traditionally, thin mortar joints are a sign of fine craft, with exceptionally skilled bricklayers able to

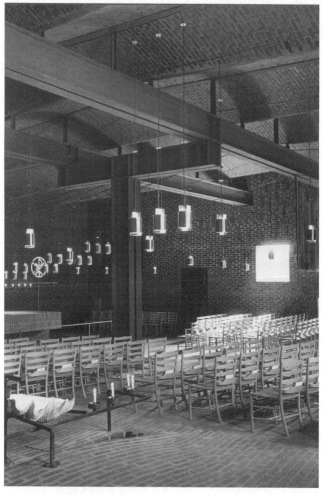

24. Church of St Peter, Klippan, Sweden, 1966. Most aspects of the church's construction were rethought afresh, although there was little attempt to be fashionable. The font is a giant reclaimed sea shell continuously dripping into a gutter in the floor. Brick vaulted ceilings were supported by a steel column and beam formed into a 'T', recalling the symbol of the cross. And windows were formed from sheets of glass simply clipped outside openings in the brick walls. (Architect: Sigurd Lewerentz.)

reduce the normal 10 millimetre joint to as little as 3 millimetres. But the brickwork at St Peter's overturns these conventions. Here, bricks swim in a soup of thick mortar—walls are more mortar than brick in places—and perpends rarely line up. Lewerentz imagined the individual bricks to symbolize individual members of the congregation, representing the body of the church, and he imagined them so precious that he declared no bricks could be cut. It was this rule which produced the unusual bricklaying logic, where mortar expands to fill spaces left between uncut bricks. Lewerentz's strange brickwork thus recalled the first Roman concrete, where masonry served as aggregate in cement. It appeared almost geological, like a natural formation, becoming what Jeremy Till later called 'the brickiest of bricks and the walliest of walls'.

Little was normal at St Peter's. While there was scant attempt to be fashionable, most aspects of the church's construction were thought afresh. Ordinary materials and details were reinvented in an attempt to imbue them with meaning. Like other buildings claimed for an alternative tradition of modern architecture in brick, the church didn't do this by returning to local architectures of the past, but instead by attempting to update traditional elements in relation to current realities of industrialization and globalization. St Peter's thus stands as a powerfully idiosyncratic illustration of the idea of another modern architecture: one imagined as an ongoing process of reinvention; retrieving specificity, meaning, and place; reclaiming history and monumentality.

Chapter 5
Light and air

Deep plans and networks

Brightly coloured 1950s American cars, dramatically styled with chrome tailfins, provided a defining image of mid-20th-century modernity. Their imagery seemed to associate modern technology with personal freedom and decadence. The future they symbolized consigned the horse and cart—then still a regular sight in the US and Europe—to the medieval past. Those ridiculous, glorious tailfins were invented by Harley Earl from General Motors (GM). And when GM sought an architect for its new 320-acre research and design campus at Warren, Michigan, on the suburban fringes of Detroit, USA, Earl helped them to choose Eero Saarinen.

GM's campus (Figure 25) was built over eight years between 1948 and 1956, at an astonishing cost for that time of $60 million. Its modern buildings tapped GM's automotive technology, burnishing the futuristic credentials of what was then America's largest corporation. A central lake was completed with artworks by modern sculptors Alexander Calder and Antoine Pevsner (no relation to Nikolaus), topped with a 40-metre tall, stainless-steel-finished water tower. Most striking was Saarinen's Styling Dome, steel clad like the cars, glinting in the sunlight like it'd landed from one of America's newly popular science-fiction (sci-fi) movies. Earl's aerodynamically styled cars were arranged in a

25. General Motors (GM) research and design campus, Warren, Michigan, USA, 1956. Its buildings tapped GM's automotive technology, burnishing the futuristic credentials of what was then America's largest corporation. A central lake was topped with a 40-metre tall, stainless-steel-finished water tower. Prominent in this photograph is the Styling Dome, glinting in the sunlight like it's landed from one of the newly popular science fiction movies. (Architect: Eero Saarinen.)

circle under the dome's reflective ceiling, and its visitors must have felt they were standing at the epicentre of the future.

The majority of buildings on GM's campus reflected modernity less sensationally. Echoing Mies's IIT campus, most comprised low-lying, pared-down, steel-framed boxes set in parkland, clad with curtain walls. Those curtain walls were flatter than Mies's, waterproofed with neoprene strips invented for another of Earl's styling innovations: the wraparound windscreen. Less immediately noticeable was the novel servicing of the GM buildings. Ceilings—like at the Technical Center Studios, 1953—told the story (Figure 26). Set-out on a 5 foot 2 inch grid, their dimensions coordinated the placement of every element from

26. Ceiling detail, Technical Center Studios, General Motors campus, Warren, Michigan, USA, 1953. The ceiling grid coordinated the placement of every element in the building, from partitions and doors to the façade glazing. It contained fluorescent tubes, electrical outlets, air supply, and air extract via concealed ducts, and fire sprinklers connected to a hidden network of pipes. (Architect: Eero Saarinen.)

partitions and doors to the façade glazing. Their regular grids brought together fluorescent tubes, electrical outlets, fire sprinklers connected to a network of pipes, and air supply and extraction via concealed ducts. Air-conditioning diffusers and sprinkler heads were placed so that partitions could be arranged and rearranged along the ceiling's grid lines. Pipes and ducts ran through the steel floor decks, with the finished ceilings hung below them as a separate element.

This 'suspended ceiling'—designed by Saarinen's office with GM technicians, plus consultants Smith Hinchman & Grylls—indicated a fresh organizing logic for modern architecture. Most buildings had previously remained relatively narrow in plan—rarely more than 12 metres across—because interior spaces had to be lit by the sun and ventilated using opening windows. Air-conditioning and fluorescent tubes, however, allowed satisfactory lighting and ventilation to be provided artificially rather than naturally. Accommodation could thus be placed further from windows, enabling buildings to become deeper in plan. This made buildings cheaper, because the amount of external wall—the most expensive part—could be reduced in relation to the overall floor area. Various office cells at GM, in the 1951 Engineering Group Building for example, had no external windows but were instead glazed boxes on internal corridors. The suspended ceiling—which since became consolidated as a global standard grid, familiar from countless offices, hospitals, and schools—stood for the substitution of natural light and air with mechanical provision. Air-conditioning and fluorescent light thus became combined to produce a deep-plan architectural logic.

American engineer Willis Haviland Carrier is credited with combining existing technologies to produce modern air-conditioning in the 1900s. Scottish chemist Joseph Black had worked out, in 1760, that heat gets absorbed when liquid evaporates into vapour, and released when vapour condenses into liquid, but the consequences were only later exploited. By the mid-19th century, American trade in ice—shipped south from northern climes for a range of uses from medical treatments to refrigerating ships' cargoes—grew so profitable that inventors started experimenting with turning water into ice mechanically using chemical refrigerants. Simultaneously, experiments were being undertaken in theatres to circulate ice- or water-cooled air—or to draw cool air from underground chambers—to reduce overheating in summer, although these were mostly ineffective or produced very humid environments. Carrier worked out that air temperature could be controlled by adjusting moisture levels: drawing air through a spray of cooled or heated vapour, supplied by coils filled with hot or cold water. He used historical weather records to calibrate temperature and moisture levels in order to mitigate excessive humidity. The resulting air-conditioning was initially used in factory spaces processing delicate materials, like celluloid film and pharmaceutical capsules. The first fully air-conditioned building was completed in 1929: the Milam Building in San Antonio, Texas, USA, where a network of ducts hung in corridors introduced cooled or warmed air into offices.

The earliest artificial lighting systems, meanwhile, burned coal gas. Gas light infrastructure became widespread in European and American cities during the late 19th century. In the 1870s, however, American engineer Charles Francis Brush developed one of the first viable systems for electric rather than gas light, connecting a steam-powered dynamo to arc lamps with copper cables. A major development was the invention and improvement of incandescent lightbulbs in the 1890s, in different forms by Thomas Edison and Joseph Swan. As power stations and electric supply networks became constructed in cities during the early 20th century (Milan was an early adopter), electric lighting overtook gas.

The precursor of modern fluorescent lighting was developed by American engineer D. McFarlan Moore, who invented an electric-powered, gas-filled, tube lamp. Different gases were tried over some forty years to produce the best illumination. Georges Claude tried neon gas in the 1910s and, although the orange light it emitted was unsuitable for lighting rooms, it made striking illuminated signs when filled into glass tubes and twisted into letters and shapes. Neon thus became a symbol of modernity and contributed to the image of International Style buildings. The 1939 New York World's Fair spurred two American companies, General Electric and Sylvania, to produce white, low voltage, fluorescent lamps. These proved phenomenally successful, shipping large volumes in the US after the Second World War. Four-fifths of the power of incandescent bulbs went to heat at that time, and only a fifth to light, with bulbs producing around 40 per cent of the cooling demand in the first air-conditioned buildings. So, fluorescent light, producing significantly less heat, became an obvious partner for air-conditioning.

By the 1950s, 'air-con' became widespread in America, not just in factories but also in theatres, offices, and rail cars, and fluorescent lighting also grew more widely employed. GM's campus illustrated an early example of their integration, combined into those highly serviced ceilings which made deep-plan buildings conceivable.

GM's campus also illustrated the translation of ideas about highly supervised, statistically analysed, mass production—like at Ford's Highland Park—from factories into offices. (Indeed, Saarinen's architect father, Eliel, knew Albert Kahn.) Deep-plan floorplates transformed office work and workplaces. Single cell offices became highly glazed, and so-called open-plan layouts were tested, arranging fields of desks and low partitions across whole floors. These 'office landscapes' allowed workers to be readily overseen, permitting the perpetual reorganization of people and furniture to suit changing management dynamics.

GM's campus was one of the first out-of-town office parks, and it illustrated changing postwar relations between home and work. The lakeside landscape was designed for viewing from a moving car, and managers assumed that employees would drive to work. The site was imagined as a gated compound on the edge of the city, connected by highway networks to workers' detached suburban houses. Due to employers like GM, Detroit became, over subsequent decades, a prime example of the movement of office work to out-of-town sites, accompanied by the movement of middle-class housing to suburbs, and shopping to roadside strip malls. Such changes transformed historic city centres in the US, some of which emptied out, leaving dereliction and poverty behind. Thus, GM's campus illustrates broader postwar shifts—found in varying degrees in different Western cultures—away from a traditional idea of civic life conducted in the streets and squares of the city towards a new preference for the private realms of office, car, home, and TV.

GM's campus also anticipated the idea of a network society. Its office workers were mostly distributed across open-plan offices, their desk layouts reflecting the network diagrams of management structures. Complex patterns of pipes, ducts, and wires embedded in the ceilings echoed complex urban networks of power and water supply. Moreover, the campus relied on its adjacent highway network, supplying goods and workers. Not long after GM's campus, Saarinen's office designed headquarters for IBM computers and Bell Telephone along similar lines. It's no coincidence that IBM's pioneering computing, soon imagined in terms of networked computers, was developed under Saarinen's networked ceilings, echoing networked urban infrastructures.

Historian Reinhold Martin has argued that these projects were connected directly into Cold War politics via 'systems thinking', which understood everything in the world as complex, interconnected, mathematically model-able systems. Martin noted the postwar Western alliance of new military technologies with commercial industrial expertise—sometimes called the 'military-industrial complex'—linking corporations with states and their armies, automotive with aeronautical design, and computing with innovations in warfare. Martin argued that the GM campus—alongside Saarinen's headquarters for IBM and Bell—stood for the global power of this 'military-industrial complex'. He illustrated the point by referring to the opening ceremony for the GM campus in 1956, dubbed 'the Versailles of Technology' by *Life* magazine after the famous French royal gardens, attended by GM's executives and their guests including senior US military officers and the president of Indonesia, addressed live from the White House by US president, Dwight D. Eisenhower. The so-called 'military-industrial complex', arguably represented by GM (who opened a Defense Division in 1950), was criticized because it profited from warfare and thus appeared perversely incentivized to promote conflict to sell technology. It was also hugely inventive, directly or indirectly spawning technologies for space travel, the microprocessor, and the networking of computers into the World Wide Web.

Test-piloting Bucky's domes

While the postwar years saw a new deep-plan architectural logic emerge from air-conditioning and artificial lighting, it had already become accepted that modern buildings should look light and airy. This imagery was helped by new glass technology which enabled the fabrication of bigger panes: so-called 'float glass', formed into continuous sheets by rolling hot liquid glass onto molten tin. Glass never produced its own architectural logic like steel and reinforced concrete had, despite experiments to design structural glass beams and columns. However, float glass did help modern architects including Mies and Corbusier to devise an imagery of lightness and airiness, and those terms became widespread in accounts of modern buildings.

This book's fourth superhero of modern architecture was the most celebrated champion of lightness in architecture: inventor, author, and 'futurologist' Richard Buckminster Fuller (1895–1983). Nicknamed 'Bucky' by fans, he was famous for delivering complex, charismatic lectures at manic speed. Born into an aristocratic Massachusetts family on America's East Coast, he became a curious blend of geek and travelling salesman, traversing the world with suitcases full of models illustrating his latest ideas. Fuller lived his life as a scientific experiment, testing all sorts of speculations, philosophies, and diets on himself—often at the expense of his long-suffering family—recording the details with astonishing comprehensiveness in a diary he named, grandly, the Dymaxion Chronofile.

Fuller was credited as a pioneer of sustainability, concerned with humanity's lasting impact on the planet, and its mitigation through technological invention. He's been depicted as a proto-Hippie, anticipating that 1960s counter-culture through his mystical ideas about destiny, 'synergistic' understanding between people, and unseen connections inherent in 'Universe'—which he wrote with a capital 'U' and without 'the', to emphasize its all-encompassing unity. Fuller talked about 'pattern integrities', phenomena evident in Universe waiting to be discovered. His example was a knot: people usually think of knots in terms of ropes, or nylon as a material, however the knot is none of those things but instead an idea that becomes form: a pattern integrity. This thinking underpinned Fuller's idealistic designs, including a three-wheeled car, future-proofed so it could later fly, 1933; a moulded copper bathroom, 1936; and a striking 'One-Ocean World' map, 1943, formulated for global citizens to design connected systems. While Fuller didn't like architects, they admired his designs for prefabricated houses—including the 4D (or Dymaxion) House, 1928–9; and Dymaxion Deployment Unit, 1940—plus an improbably lightweight structural system he invented called Tensegrity, 1948, and super-light 'geodesic' domes, 1949.

Various modern architects, like Saarinen, were entranced by possibilities for factory production, and so-called technology-transfer from the automobile industry, fantasizing about mass-producing 'prefabricated' houses ready for delivery to site. Fuller's Dymaxion House fulfilled these fantasies. As historian Mark Wigley has noted, Fuller became frustrated by the wastefulness of houses in relation to the 'magical efficiency' of new technologies like cars and radios. In response, Fuller argued in 1929 that houses should: eliminate domestic work, exploitation, selfishness, and centralized control; safeguard against flood, storms, fire, earthquakes, hurricanes, and marauders; and save time for education, amusement, and advancement. He invented the term Dymaxion—which he applied to various inventions—for publicity purposes, emphasizing futuristic-sounding words, combining 'dynamic' and 'maximum' with the scientific 'ion'.

Fuller's proposed Dymaxion House, presented in striking drawings and models in 1928–9, was to be factory made and delivered by airship. Dramatically, the airship would drop a bomb to form a crater in the ground. The house—centred on a mast containing staircase, lift, and electrical and mechanical services—would then be lowered into the hole, like planting a tree, and concreted-in, with tension wires added to secure it. Driven by solar and wind power—also recycling rainwater, and packaging solid waste for reprocessing—the house could exist off-grid in remote areas, or indeed in cities, ready for immediate inhabitation.

Fuller's house anticipated numerous future technologies, several commercialized only later in the century, and numerous components were thought afresh. Many innovations made novel use of air-conditioning, provided to remove smells and dust, and also to pressurize air for other uses. The structure was designed as a lightweight aluminium frame set out on a triangular grid, infilled with translucent vacuum-sealed panels and fitted with springy inflatable floors. Pneumatic silk partitions and doors were accompanied by plug-in vacuum hoses and inflatable furniture whose firmness could be controlled by the users. The ceiling was conceived as a continuous surface admitting diffuse light, with vents to control temperature. Furniture would be suspended from this ceiling, including glass tables on neon-lit cables. Storage would be provided in revolving units. Triangular curtains, fitting the structural module, would pull out of the floor or drop from the ceiling. A moulded bathroom unit, in the mast, would wash people instantly with an atomized spray. A utility space, which Fuller dubbed the 'catch-up-with-life room', would clean and dry clothes within minutes. A 'go-ahead-with-life room' would contain a radio, television (barely viable technology at the time), maps, globes, revolving book shelves, a drawing board, typewriter, and various learning materials. Fuller imagined residents of Dymaxion Houses as planetary citizens liberated from domestic drudge by technology, freed up to dream and invent as active contributors to 'Spaceship Earth' (a term he coined later, in 1951).

Fuller claimed that the Dymaxion House could be produced by an automobile company and cost as little as a car. Like the cars and personal aeroplanes shown parked beneath it in drawings, he envisaged that it could be easily moved. When residents wanted to relocate, they could take their house with them. Fuller never saw a Dymaxion House built at full size—blaming the entrenched interests of the architectural establishment for opposing mass production—but his models inspired diverse imagery in architecture, art, fiction, and film, including interiors in sci-fi movies as diverse as (the hugely sexist) *Barbarella*, 1968, and *Star Wars*, 1977.

Life under a dome

While Fuller never saw a Dymaxion House built, deployable shelters were constructed to his designs for US military use during the Cold War. One memorable image shows a lightweight dome suspended from a helicopter with a single cable. That dome was part of a twenty-year research project conducted with students whom Fuller taught as visiting professor at a sequence of universities.

These 'geodesic domes' were highly efficient spheres—or, more usually, part-spheres—inspired by bugs' eyes and spiders' webs, made from slender structural elements arranged in triangles. Developed through a mix of complex mathematics and trial and error, they employed the least material possible, arranged in the most efficient way, to transmit loads to the ground. Geodesic domes seemed impossibly light and strong. An image of the second prototype—made by students at Black Mountain College, North Carolina in 1949—shows people hanging improbably off a lightweight frame (Figure 27).

27. **Geodesic dome prototype, Black Mountain College, USA, 1949. Geodesic domes were inspired by bugs' eyes and spiders' webs, made from slender structural elements arranged in triangles employing the least material possible, in the most efficient way, to transmit loads to the ground. Students hang improbably from this prototype which they had constructed. (Designer: Buckminster Fuller.)**

Fuller led the construction of prototype domes at Montreal, Canada, in 1951, North Carolina State College, 1952, and the University of Oregon, 1953, before the awarding of a patent in 1954. He had domestic applications in mind, making a detailed model of what he called the Skybreak House in 1952. This showed a bubble-like alloy dome, lifted on stilts, finished with a lightweight transparent insulating plastic skin. Furniture would be arranged on a platform at the base of the dome and only the most private functions would be separated out into enclosed boxes. Fuller enthused that transparent domes like this would dissolve the traditional idea of the house, likening them to living under the sky. Wall and roof, here, were to be combined into an almost-invisible layer of high performance plastic. While no such plastic was viable at that time, Fuller and his student collaborators tested several innovative materials including Mylar, receiving free samples from DuPont and other corporations.

Most of the geodesic domes realized were commissioned by the US military. In 1949, Fuller installed a prototype at The Pentagon, Washington, DC—headquarters of the US Department of Defense—for use in conflicts and disaster-relief. Another dome—a lightweight timber lattice covered in chicken wire, with a sprayed-on neoprene rubber skin, built by North Carolina State University students—was the one that was test-lifted by a US Marines helicopter in 1951. The experiment was deemed a success, and lightweight magnesium-framed domes were then commissioned from Fuller's company, Geodesics Inc., for military applications. In 1955, a dome made in fibreglass was tested on the roof of the Lincoln Laboratory at MIT, Cambridge, Massachusetts, to cover an experimental radar installation, proving invisible to the radar, and surviving a hurricane shortly afterwards. Wise to a marketing opportunity, Fuller branded this variant the 'Radome', photographing workers balancing its triangular components on their fingertips to illustrate their lightness and strength. When a line of sixty-three radar stations was constructed in 1957 at the frozen extremity of the Americas to provide early warning of Soviet invasion, from Alaska to Baffin Island, they were covered with 'Bucky Domes'. As Wigley remarked, the geodesic dome 'no longer simply defined just...domestic shelter', it defined 'domestic security for an entire continent'.

Fuller spent a lifetime fascinated by experimental materials, excited by futuristic imagery, imagining buildings made for delivery by airship and helicopter. He challenged assumptions that architecture should be heavyweight, fixed, and expensive. Visiting a building designed by British architects Norman and Wendy Foster in 1978, he enquired memorably: 'How much does your building weigh?' Fuller implied: why shouldn't buildings be cheap and portable? Why shouldn't they provide technological liberations like those offered by cars and televisions? His structures went beyond the idea that modern architecture ought simply to look light and airy to realizing highly lightweight, almost transparent structures. Indeed, his anti-architectural, anti-establishment thinking inspired a diverse group of architects, critics, engineers, and 'drop outs' in the 1960s and 1970s.

Bubbles and blimps

Fuller's geodesics proposed stripping architecture back to basic human shelter. In a 1960 book, *Theory and Design in the First Machine Age*, Banham (again) argued that form never really did follow function in 'International Style' modernism. Its buildings offered superficial images of modernity, he argued, but didn't tap the full potential of new technologies. In the spirit of Fuller, and Mies's dictum that 'less is more', Banham argued that mechanical and electrical services—artificial lighting, air-conditioning, and power supply—represented the basic components of shelter, ideally supplemented only by the most minimal of enclosures.

A 1965 article by Banham in the magazine *Art in America* was illustrated by artist François Dallegret. Together, they proposed 'The Unhouse'. Dallegret's section depicted a double-skinned, inflated transparent plastic bubble on a plinth, showing a group of greyed-out naked Banhams and Dallegrets collaged around a central technological 'totem-pole'. That totem held lamps, a TV screen, stereo speakers, fridge, cooker, and air supply. Meanwhile, the architecture became reduced to two thin lines representing plastic membranes. The proposal was inspired by technologies then being developed for early space exploration, for the artificial environmental bubbles of rocket ships and space suits. Banham and Dallegret described the Unhouse as a 'living package' that would do away with the weighty encumbrances of buildings, and their associated social and cultural baggage, indicating new ways of life. The naked figures in the drawing referred to the 1960s idea of sexual liberation, supposedly occasioned by the newly invented female contraceptive pill. They also referred to 'primitive man' [*sic*], proposing a return to an idea about architecture's ancient origins: a circle of people gathered around a fire, as described in the oldest surviving architecture book—Vitruvius' *De Architectura*, 1st century CE.

Several designers explored this reduction of architecture to clear, inflated plastic membranes. Examples included: Michael Webb's experimental 'Cushicle' bubble, and his plastic 'Suitaloon' fitted to the human body, 1967; Haus-Rucker-Co's (self-explanatory) 'Balloon for Two', also 1967; 'Mobile Office', an inflated drum where the architect Hans Hollein sat at a drawing board, 1969; Ant Farm's 'Clean Air Pod', 1970; and the 'Restless Sphere' that the Austrian collective Co-op Himmelb(l)au rolled around the streets of Basel, Switzerland, 1971. In such projects, membranes became second skins for human figures, whose blurry contours appeared through their surface reflections. These architects took lightness and airiness to an extreme at a time when Tange and Safdie were simultaneously designing heavyweight megastructures, and Kahn was seeking a new monumentality for modern architecture. In contrast, their anti-monumental projects questioned whether architecture should involve buildings at all. These inflatable fantasies deliberately challenged architecture's traditional associations with permanence. But their designers also diverged somewhat from Banham and Dallegret's vision of the Unhouse: they understood their bubbles not as an extension of total environmental control—as proposed by Banham, and as embodied in Saarinen's GM campus where fluorescent lighting and air-conditioning substituted for natural light and air—but instead as a parody of total environmental control. The inhabitants of these bubbles were not imagined as enclosed by technology, so much as imprisoned by it.

A spirit of satire informed these young architects' work, partly in response to the counter-culture of the late 1960s and early 1970s. Various anti-establishment movements first flourished across Europe and the US in association with the coming-of-age of the postwar 'baby boomers'. They played to the soundtrack of the Beatles and Rolling Stones, relaxed with (what Banham called) 'wonder-drugs and new domestic chemistries', championed equal rights for all genders and ethnicities, and looked up to a new creative class of celebrities, artists, and designers. 'Hippie' incarnations of these movements in the late 1960s reacted specifically against the Vietnam War and the draft of young Americans to fight. Their thinking endorsed a new environmentalism—as highlighted by Fuller—acutely aware of the fragility of planet Earth and the destruction of life by human activity. Student groups associated with the counter-culture were highly political, imagining mainstream figures—including their teachers—as a complacent, reactionary establishment. Their frustrations boiled over into demonstrations in 1968—in Paris, New York, Prague, and West Berlin, for example—challenging what they saw as the imperial ambitions of warmongering anti-democratic regimes, championing instead freedom and civil rights. These demonstrations—some violently suppressed—didn't represent a coherent global movement, but they did connect local, national, and international concerns with wider protest and trade union groups.

Some radicals decided to 'drop out' of mainstream society, to reject the establishment and money culture, collecting together to live communal subsistence lives. In 1965, four art students—styled as Curly, Jo, Lard, and Clard—founded a commune in remote southeast Colorado, USA, self-building geodesic domes out of recycled components like car parts. Another group—Ant Farm, whose chief protagonists were architects Chip Lord and Doug Michaels—began building a so-called nomadic environment in Death Valley, California, with domes and inflatables, working with the writer Stewart Brand. Brand's *Whole Earth Catalog*, several editions of which were published between 1968 and 1971, mixed articles about self-sufficiency, ecology, and radical education with reviews of building products and DIY (do-it-yourself) tips. It provided a 'how-to' guide for alternative living. Steve Jobs—who founded the Homebrew Computer Club in California before founding Apple Computers—later described it as 'like Google in paperback form, 35 years before Google'. Jobs highlighted that, while communes never became mainstream, they incubated ideas about sharing and information economies that later informed the emerging Internet.

Mainstream postwar modern architecture gradually became seen as part of the establishment problem. It got associated with top-down comprehensive redevelopment involving the clearance of settled communities—for example, the imposition of housing and office blocks constructed in the West in the 1960s on the lines of Corbusier's Ville Contemporaine—driven by local and national authorities. This growing perception was strengthened by author, activist, and sociologist Jane Jacobs's 1961 book *Death and Life of Great American Cities*. Jacobs studied lively traditional neighbourhoods with strong communities and a vibrant street life, including Boston's North End, then slated to be cleared, showing how they figured better in health, crime, and education measures than replacement modern neighbourhoods.
Such perceived failures of modern architecture became symbolized by the demolition of the troubled Pruitt-Igoe housing blocks in St Louis, Missouri, USA, in 1972. Memorable images of their demolition illustrated a growing disillusionment with modern architecture, which became perceived as an accessory of top-down control. The bubbles of Banham, Co-op Himmelb(l)au,

Drop City, and others can be understood in this context as a rejection of centralized planning and industrial construction; conceived instead as recovering the supposed early promise of modern architecture to express straightforwardly new technologies and new social configurations.

Rightly or wrongly, the fantastical drawings of the Archigram group became seen as defining images of 1960s counter-culture. Archigram began as a group of British students and architects comprising Michael Webb (whose Cushicle and Suitaloon have been mentioned earlier), Warren Chalk, Peter Cook, Dennis Crompton, David Greene, and Ron Herron. The name 'Archigram' combined 'architecture' with 'telegram', then the fastest means of global communication (a kind of text message sent from post offices). They used the same name for an anti-architecture fanzine they published on a shoestring budget, containing memorable images that mashed-up clip-outs from advertising and film posters with sci-fi comic imagery and straight-laced technical drawing. Historian Simon Sadler has shown how these drawings blended humour with seriousness, experimental fantasies with plausible technological predictions, techno-gadgetry with ideas about disposableness, and 1960s radical politics with the macho derring-do of boys' comics.

Herron's drawing for 'Walking City', 1964, proposed giant insect-inspired megastructures on eight legs: alternative communities made of prefabricated modules that could stride across the landscape. Dennis Crompton's 'Computor City' drawings, 1964, showed an abstract grid of dwellings looking like substations and diodes, plugged-in with pipes and cables, expressing the idea of the city as a connected network. Most memorable was Peter Cook's cartoon strip proposing an 'Instant City', 1969. Emblazoned with slogans, the images illustrated successive stages for the take over of a 'sleeping' small town. First, an airship would arrive and get plugged in. Then it would lower tents and billboards to provoke spontaneous events, enlivening the town's spaces (Figure 28). 'Square becomes theatre', the drawing proclaims, 'yard about to become disco-talkpit', and the blimp drops projection screens. After a period of 'high intensity', the airship would move on, leaving a town infiltrated with 'learning stations' and 'infocentre' technology. Ongoing 'counter-action' would then be inspired among empowered young people, the Instant City network having taken over.

Archigram's drawings followed Fuller's lead in claiming a spontaneous, playful, and disposable architecture. They conceived architecture as short-term rather than long-term, as the design of transient events rather than fixed structures. Indeed, the combination of technology, culture, and democracy they illustrated resonated afresh with a later generation grappling with how to imagine the newly popularized Internet in the 2000s.

EVENT

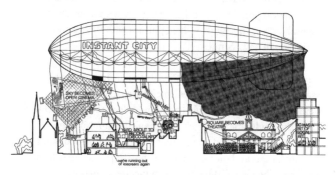

28. Instant City Airships, 1969. Stage three of a sequence showing the effect on a typical English town. 'Square becomes theatre', 'yard about to become disco-talkpit', and the blimp drops projection screens. After a period of 'high intensity', the airship moves on, leaving behind ongoing 'counter-action' inspired by empowered young people. (Drawing: Peter Cook and Archigram.)

Skin and guts

The closest anyone got to building Instant City, or something like it, was in Paris's Marais district. A competition, held in 1971, sought architects for a gallery, library, and contemporary music labs. The jury—chaired by Jean Prouvé, an engineer famous for demountable structures—chose a design from a then-obscure duo: Renzo Piano and Richard Rogers, working with engineers Ove Arup & Partners. In the spirit of the 1968 protests, Piano and Rogers proposed an anti-institutional institution. The building that finally opened in 1978—named Centre Georges Pompidou after the French president who championed it, and often called Beaubourg after its site—contained all the contradictions you might expect of an expensive, permanent, state-sponsored institution trying to seem temporary, spontaneous, and radical.

Beaubourg brought together the deep-plan logic of air-conditioning and fluorescent lighting with ideas of spontaneity evoked by Archigram's bubbles and blimps. It comprised a substantial steel frame, supporting broad, highly serviced free-plan floorplates without intermediate columns. These floorplates, it was imagined, would provide maximum flexibility for radical curators to stage events: combining painting and sculpture with video and sound art, for example, or altogether new art forms. It was originally proposed that floor segments should move up and down for extra flexibility, although this was later abandoned because of cost, along with digital billboards proposed for the façades. Escalators were threaded through the structural frame in glazed tubes on one façade, facing a new public square, offering striking views over Paris, and symbolizing dynamism and spontaneity. The primary street façade, meanwhile, comprised a web of brightly coloured pipes and ducts, feeding service voids in the suspended ceilings and raised floors behind (Figure 29). Putting the ducts on the outside helped keep the floorplates free of disruptive service zones. But it also conferred the building a radically novel image—a

29. Pompidou Centre, Beaubourg, Paris, France, 1978. The street façade comprises a web of brightly coloured pipes and ducts, set in the structural frame, feeding service voids in the suspended ceilings and raised floors behind. Putting the ducts on the outside helped keep the huge floorplates free of disruptive service zones, expressing structure and servicing technology dramatically. Historians dubbed this architectural imagery 'high-tech'. (Architects: Renzo Piano and Richard Rogers.)

dramatized expression of structure and servicing technology—which historians subsequently categorized as its own architectural style: 'high-tech'.

Beaubourg's attempts to express informality and spontaneity weren't so original, drawing from: Banham's idea of architecture as a serviced container; Archigram's imagery; the 19th-century engineering of Paxton and Eiffel; and a 1960s proposal for a flexible 'Fun Palace' in London, imagined by theatre director

Joan Littlewood with architect Cedric Price. It was distinguished from comparable proposals, however, by the fact of getting built, albeit with compromises: the escalator tubes later became privatized, incorporated into the paid-for gallery 'experience' rather than free to the public, and curators later built permanent rooms on certain floorplates to save the cost of refitting them for every exhibition.

When it was finished, Beaubourg was as unpopular with the Parisian elite as Eiffel's tower had been a century before. The philosopher Jean Baudrillard thought it illustrated: 'the image of a culture flattened by its own weight', 'generated...by logicians of the establishment wholly lacking in critical spirit'. Beaubourg sold out its radical potential, he believed, by freezing promises of dynamism and spontaneity into a fixed institution. Moreover—with unashamed elitism—Baudrillard criticized Beaubourg as being a machine to mass produce art for the masses. He abhorred how its imagery—expressing the guts of its building services—honoured mass production more than it honoured the cultures of artistic craft. To Baudrillard, Beaubourg rejected the idea of artistic endeavour as the pinnacle of human thought and civilization—which he thought a cultural building should celebrate—standing instead for banal industrial modernity.

Before partnering with Piano, Richard Rogers—and Su Rogers—had worked with fellow British architects Norman and Wendy Foster. The Fosters, practising as Foster Associates, completed another art gallery—the Sainsbury Centre, at the University of East Anglia, Norwich, UK—in 1978. At first glance, it looked like the no-nonsense steel roadside sheds familiar across America or Europe. 'Ugly ordinary' roadside buildings had been celebrated in Robert Venturi, Denise Scott Brown, and Stephen Izenour's 1971 book *Learning from Las Vegas*. But the Sainsbury Centre became a refined, exaggerated version of those everyday sheds, sited on a rise in the landscape like an ancient temple (Figure 30).

30. Sainsbury Centre, University of East Anglia, Norwich, UK, 1978.
A double-skin 'space frame' containing structure, services, and
secondary rooms was lined inside and out with bespoke engineered
panels—louvered, glazed, and ribbed aluminium-covered—sealed with
neoprene gaskets to produce a sleek skin. The shed's ends—equally
sleek glass walls, supported on glass fins—are over-sailed by the space
frame to form porticoes. (Architects: Foster Associates.)

It had a so-called 'space frame' structure—inspired by Fuller's
geodesics, made of slender steel tubes formed into interlocking
triangles—concealed in wide double skins. These double
skins contained substantial spaces for structure, services,
and maintenance gantries, and even secondary rooms like WCs
and storerooms. Between the two double skins was a vast room
for exhibitions without any intermediate columns, 30 metres
wide, 7.5 metres high and 130 metres long. Two mezzanine levels
for the university's fine artists, plus a basement for delivery,
workshop and conservation areas, freed up this single volume to
contain only mobile screens and vitrines for artworks. The double
skins were lined inside and out with a mixture of bespoke
engineered panels—ribbed, aluminium-covered, louvred,
and glazed—sealed with neoprene gaskets to produce a sleek

134

surface. In theory, those panels, each fixed with only six bolts, could be reconfigured to suit changes in interior layout. The shed's short ends, meanwhile, comprised equally sleek glass walls, supported on glass fins, over-sailed by the space frame to form porticoes overlooking the landscape.

Beaubourg and the Sainsbury Centre were both conceived as highly serviced containers of art. But their architectural imagery diverged. The first expressed the guts of its structure and servicing—beams, pipes, ducts, and lifts—while the second concealed the same servicing inside a sleek double skin, revealing it only in tantalizing glimpses through glazed panels. Both sought an imagery of light and air. Both highlighted the complex structure and servicing required to build sports-hall-like spaces for art. Both traded on the rhetoric of flexibility and spontaneity. However—as illustrated by the permanent rooms retrofitted to Beaubourg's floorplates, and reconfigurable panels at the Sainsbury Centre that were never reconfigured—both also overstated their flexibility. These 'high-tech' buildings were set apart from Saarinen's GM campus and Fuller's geodesics by their visual exaggeration of their technological credentials—illustrated by technicolour ducts and a double skin containing significantly more space than strictly necessary.

Previous modern buildings I've discussed in this book questioned the merits of architectural decoration, understood by their architects as arbitrary, unnecessary, and morally wrong. But Beaubourg and the Sainsbury Centre, by contrast, renewed concern for amplified imagery. They moved beyond ideas about deriving plan form, for example, and the placement of windows, straightforwardly from functional necessities. They didn't only express technology, they 'fetishized' it (as critics said at the time). Beaubourg's web of ducts became a kind of ornamentation. As did the sleek surfaces of the Sainsbury Centre, artfully caricaturing ordinary roadside sheds, and expensively reinventing typical components. Both buildings took the expression of technology beyond, say, E.1027 or Seagram, and beyond the rhetoric of functional logic. Previous modern buildings *emphasized* technology visually, where Beaubourg and Sainsbury artfully *exaggerated* it, engaging in technologically inspired embellishment.

This distinction is subtle but important. It shows how Beaubourg and Sainsbury extended the functional ethos of modern design but also went beyond it. Arguably, these buildings rejected Ruskin's insistence on truth to materials by accentuating functional necessities for visual effect, flouting Loos's insistence that 'ornament is a crime' and Mies's dictum that 'less is more'.

These buildings' complex imagery reflected the growing complexities of the time. The 1973 Energy Crisis—when Middle Eastern oil companies refused to supply fuel to certain Western countries because of a war with Israel—highlighted connections between burgeoning oil consumption, global politics, and ecological concerns. The crisis highlighted the fragility of energy supply at a time when its reliability had become taken for granted. It renewed postwar apprehensions about the value of technology for society. And it coincided with a prolonged economic downturn causing the decline of established industries, and communities around them, in the West. Meanwhile, the Cold War threat of imminent nuclear destruction persisted.

A growing popular sense emerged that the modern promise of perpetual progress—linking technology and democracy with ever-increasing living standards—had halted. Art, literature, and film increasingly reflected this emerging scepticism. Meanwhile, prominent philosophers and cultural theorists challenged the fundamental basis of scientific and technological thinking. They illustrated how the supposedly objective realities, and absolute truths, of science and technology conveniently reflected the values of a prosperous, white, Western, male elite. Feminism, civil rights, ecological activism, and studies of global power ('postcolonialism') highlighted links between global finance, political authority, and the priorities of industry and military technologies, questioning the motivations of the powerful global technocratic establishment. It's now widely assumed that modernity came to an end in the 1980s and 1990s because of this growing loss of faith in the ideas of progress and technology, highlighting the increasingly complicated problems of so-called developed societies. These complexities can be seen reflected in the subtle, if fundamental, shift from modern architectures which expressed technology to those like Beaubourg and Sainsbury which heightened it.

Beaubourg and Sainsbury were transitional. They remained statements of faith in the social promise of technology. But, as philosopher Walter Benjamin reflected, every age dreams its successor, and their 'high-tech' imagery also anticipated the so-called postmodern architecture of the 1980s, which rejected modern moralizing about honest architectural expression, and re-embraced heightened imagery. While the underlying structural logic of postmodern buildings usually remained straightforwardly modern, their surfaces became ornamented with decoration derived from architectural history, swooping or jagged 'deconstructed' forms or, indeed, high-tech motifs. Thus, Beaubourg and Sainsbury stand *both* for late modernity *and* the emergence of what followed. They conclude this story about modern architecture. However, they could equally begin another story about postmodern architecture.

Chapter 6
Conclusion

Bessemer steel, Portland cement, concrete reinforcement, and electric light—all key technical ingredients of architectural modernity—were products of the 19th century. The distinctive architectural moralities concerning 'truth' to materials and functions, which became associated with them, were also consolidated in the 19th century, deriving from the theories of Ruskin, Semper, Viollet-le-Duc, and others. Their future combination into what later became recognized as modern architecture was not obvious at the time. It looked inevitable only in retrospect, when historians like Russell-Hitchcock, Pevsner, and Banham—with their own agendas—arranged buildings and ideas into coherent stories. It took until the first half of the 20th century for architects to mature their ideas, in conjunction with new materials, into the distinctive imagery that's now recognized as modern architecture. But that imagery was only the outward sign of new ways of organizing structure, space, and surface: integrating architecture with services; exploring novel logics of frames and planes; and testing free- and open-plans.

Modern architects only gradually learnt to talk about their designs in today's familiar terms, emphasizing function, simplicity, order, space, place, light, and air. That emerging vocabulary didn't encourage them to discuss what their buildings looked like. Nor did it help them to acknowledge their intertextual references to art, engineering, or industrial design. Instead, most modern architects promoted the myth that their buildings' appearance was merely a consequence of functional planning, and the organizational logics inherent in the materials they employed.

Many *post*modern architects, however, remembered that—just like the Iron Bridge was shaped as an arch because that's what bridges were expected to look like—people maintained deep-seated preferences about how buildings should appear. Despite efforts, by Mies for example, to design definitive modern college and office buildings, most people's preferred architectural imagery remained premodern, and specific to familiar cultures. According to postmodern theorists, notably Léon Krier, these preferences were related to particular building types, like houses, schools, or hospitals. For example, in Britain, the lasting popular image of the house seems to have remained in brick or stone, with a pitched roof and pretty decorative porch. In West German cities, the image of home remains flats in courtyard blocks, with their particular pattern of communal living. It seemed that people were most comfortable with the imagery of modern architecture only in building types most closely associated with modern technologies, like railway stations, car parks, and motorway service areas. In the 1980s, this thinking chimed with ideas from the study of language, from 'semiotics', which examined how the word-labels attached to things remain separate from the things themselves. Why do we call a tree a *tree*, semioticians asked (or an *árbol* or a 树), and not a *kudfgaefjkd*? Similarly, postmodern architects speculated about the appearance of architecture in terms of visual languages. What, for example, makes a mosque look like a mosque and not a garage?

Some modern architects—such as Aalto, Carlo Scarpa, or George Pace—abstracted traditional architectural forms to produce modern ones which nevertheless seemed familiar, making intertextual references to older architectures. But *post*modern architects instead frequently covered their buildings with façades that pasted in traditional 'signifying' forms. For example, big urban buildings like shopping malls were frequently collaged with a variety of historic (or historic-ish) elevations to make them look like traditional city blocks comprising multiple buildings. Modern architects would have dismissed this as inauthentic, concealing the inherent logic of the building and its materials. The engineering behind postmodern façades like these usually remained stubbornly modern, however, comprising steel and concrete frames optimized to suit the building's functions. In numerous examples like this, ghosts of modern architecture—in the traces of modern ideas and organizational logics—have remained tenaciously persistent.

Ghosts of modern architecture

The current strand of expert architectural practice which subscribes most closely to modern values is digital design, often called 'parametricism' because it sometimes employs computer modelling to test design parameters. Its architects continue to pursue new technologies towards distinctive imagery, but they work with technologies of design process more than novel materials. Innovative software allows such architects to model extraordinarily elaborate shapes. In parallel, experimental manufacturing has transformed the fantasy of mass production into a new fantasy of 'mass customization', where elaborate shapes can be fabricated from individual components mass produced digitally as one-offs. Examples include projects from the offices of NOX, Jürgen Mayer, Zaha Hadid Architects, and Gehry Partners.

Ghosts of ideas about truth to materials and function remain—through their rejection—in projects by OMA with Rem Koolhaas: extensions to IIT's Mies-designed Commons building, 2003, for example; and Casa da Música, Porto, Portugal, 2005. These projects matched cheap materials with crude fixings, rejecting the obsessive detailing of Mies and Lewerentz, whose apparently simple elements required huge effort to make. OMA did this both to critique modern architecture and to illustrate how present-day concerns—like increased developer profits, mass-produced building components, and diminishing craft skills—mean that architectural detailing, as once understood, can seem largely impossible. OMA's deliberately 'bad' details remain as considered, however, as any they criticize.

The plans of famous modern buildings could often be summarized in simple organizational diagrams, so-called 'parti sketches', like Mies's Crown Hall—a steel pavilion sat on a base—or Kahn's Yale Center for Fine Art—a stack of floorplates punctured with vertical volumes. Another strand of contemporary practice emphasizes clear, if not always so straightforwardly functional, plan or section diagrams. Kazuyo Sejima + Ryue Nishizawa/SANAA's Learning Centre in Lausanne, Switzerland, 2010, provides an example, conceived as a giant free-plan space sandwiched between undulating floor and roof planes with circular courtyards drilled through. MVRDV's Market Hall, Rotterdam, 2014, enclosed stalls under a vast hoop of flats. Such projects are defined by the logic of their diagrams, which control characteristic aspects of the architecture.

The idea of regionalism—associated with Gut Garkau Farm and Säynätsalo Town Hall—persists among architects who seek to adapt forces of globalized construction to local conditions, pursuing contemporary national architectures. Such thinking underpins otherwise hugely divergent designs from the offices of Wang Shu and Lu Wenyu in China, for example, Rogelio Salmona in Colombia, and Glenn Murcutt in rural Australia.

Ideas from the 1960s counter-culture also persist. Ongoing interest in self-build is exemplified by projects facilitated in Chile by architects Elemental, and in Burkina Faso by Diébédo Francis Kéré. Evidence about climate change caused by human activity has renewed Fuller's concerns about the urgency of ecological design. Responses range from technological approaches—inventing devices to reduce the energy consumption of other devices, as in the 'eco-tech' practice of T.R. Hamzah & Yeang from Malaysia, and later work from Foster's office—to those rejecting complex technologies—like buildings at the Centre for Alternative Technology, Machynlleth, Wales.

Various strands of contemporary practice, occasionally called 'neo-modern', trade in the imagery of modern architecture without subscribing so strictly to its moralities. Examples include the 'crafted boxes' of Gigon Guyer's practice in Switzerland, and the white architectures of Álvaro Siza and Eduardo Souto da Moura in Portugal enlivened with thoughtful, whimsical details. Similarly, Peter Zumthor's sensory modern architecture enriches simple forms with evocative materials to engender emotive atmospheres. Such projects aspire to the imagery of truth to materials without necessarily achieving it, seeking to maintain the illusion of simple construction after new regulatory regimes have made architectural simplicity significantly harder to achieve.

Regulation and risk

It might seem curious to turn to the emergence of building regulations in concluding this book, but they were decisive in both the demise of modern imagery, and the simultaneous consolidation of modern values in the present-day construction industry.

Building regulations multiplied in most Western countries during the latter part of the 20th century as a cultural consequence of the forces of industrial production. Regulatory regimes burgeoned in a postwar context of state paternalism and increasing professionalization, seeking to regularize non-professionals, and to protect the public from excesses of profit-driven developers, consultants, and landlords. They also responded to a loss of construction skills following an increasing decline in architectural ornamentation. This decline diminished cultures of craft and artisanal care in building, alongside a corresponding proliferation of industrial building products—including window, door, and roofing components—understood as technical systems. Clients increasingly began to insist upon the warranties that came with such systems, giving architects increasingly fewer opportunities to invent evocative details—like Aalto did—progressively rendering designers as shoppers for, and coordinators of, mass-produced parts.

Building regulations progressively made modernism unworkable at the level of detail. Increasing requirements for greater insulation necessitated ever more complex interfaces between components, serving to thicken-up previously simple, slender connections. Likewise, structural rules required additional factors of safety in steel and concrete sizing, frustrating the imagery of lightness. Also, certain accessibility regulations have dictated contrasting surfaces to assist people with visual impairments, outlawing visual simplicity by multiplying textures and colours—additionally prohibiting the modern detail where wall materials continue as floor materials, as at St Peter's, Klippan.

In contrast, however, building regulation regimes have also consolidated other priorities of modern architecture. They usually required the submission of structural calculations, which had the effect of promoting steel and concrete frames—that engineers find easier to analyse—over timber and masonry. They have often specified consistent light levels—in classrooms and offices for example—requiring artificial lighting even where windows are present because natural light is deemed too unreliable for healthy screen use. Similarly, rules quantifying the number of air changes needed per hour in certain spaces have frequently discounted natural ventilation as unpredictable, dictating mechanical air handling. Regulations like these deal largely in technical performance and, as such, their values clearly derive from modern architecture—focused on function, with little to say about what buildings look and feel like.

These values inherent in building regulation regimes resonate with the current international construction industry. Fuelled by global finance, consuming mass-produced building products, resourced by multinational consultants, that industry has become highly risk-averse. It tends to prefer quantitative data about the timely and profitable delivery of buildings over wearisome considerations about their visual qualities, cultural meanings, and atmospheres. Indeed, surveyors, project managers, and engineers—frequently more adept than architects in the language of reliable delivery, like Paxton and Eiffel more than a century before—have assumed the bulk of project management from architects in numerous national contexts. Thus, innovative architectural imagery has regularly become understood as unnecessarily risky. Architects—preoccupied with design ideas, frequently more concerned with the qualities of finished buildings than management processes used to deliver them—can struggle to get heard in contemporary construction. Dominant industry values have become so unshakeably modern—rooted in technical criteria, ambivalent to visual, social, and atmospheric qualities—that architects, many of whom now question modern priorities, can regularly feel they don't belong.

Multiple modernities

In retrospect, it's easy to caricature modern architecture as symbolizing the idea of modernity as an unquestioned good: promoting technology, industry, and novelty as progress; celebrating the globalization of trade, finance, and culture. It's also easy to caricature, in opposition, a renewed preference for traditional architectures—romanticizing a return to historical motifs, local materials, and time-honoured crafts—as symbolizing a rejection of modernity in favour of reclaiming a sentimental idea of the pre-industrial past. However, these positions are false opposites. Modernity and modern architecture were always double-edged. The popular uptake of new technologies was always accompanied by anxieties about the effects of industrialization and globalization. These contradictions were exemplified by the medieval imagery of suburban villas constructed by British developers in the 1930s, which were nevertheless kitted-out with electric light, radios, telephones, and kitchen devices. Over time, there have been numerous global equivalents of these houses, fitting versions of Fuller's technological environments inside traditional-looking architectural cloaks. Architects and critics, schooled in modern ideas about architecture as an honest reflection of the age, usually scorn them. But such buildings stand as preliminary attempts to reconcile modernity with previous cultures and priorities of everyday life, just like the architectures of Aalto, Kahn, and Lewerentz did more artfully. They reflect complex, provisional settlements between ideas of future and past, progress and history, global and local, industrial and pastoral, universal and particular, individual and civic, and mass produced and artisan. They stand, awkwardly, for the simultaneous popular acceptance and rejection of modernity and its priorities. The continuing prevalence of such architectures illustrates ongoing difficulties in grasping what modernity was, and negotiating what its implications continue to be. It's clear that, for much of the 20th century, modern architecture stood for the place of the future—as related to the past—in the present. But the associations of those ideas about future, present, and past always remained complex, changing, and contested.

For all its global effects, modernity was never a unified phenomenon. Aspects of the experience of modernity were shared, characterized by new technologies which accelerated change in urbanization, work, and domestic life. However, modernity was experienced differently by different people in different places at different times: hardly the same in Soviet Romania as in Canada, or at the end of the 18th century as in the middle of the 20th. Indeed, it felt different depending on the opportunities, or lack of them, afforded by people's wealth, class, gender, and ethnicity. Just as experiences of modernity were complex and diverse, so the famous modern buildings I've introduced here had ideas in common and others that separated them. In various ways, however, they all exhibited faith in the social promise of technology. They celebrated architectural innovation, imagining that a changed architecture was necessary to represent a changed world, at a time when the rate of social and industrial change kept increasing. Their images expressed optimism that modernity could transform people's lives for the better. And there were times and places when that optimism seemed infectious.

References

General

Cecil D. Elliott, *Technics and Architecture: The Development of Materials and Systems for Buildings* (Cambridge, MA: MIT Press, 1994).
Adrian Forty, *Words and Buildings: A Vocabulary of Modern Architecture* (London: Thames and Hudson, 2004).
Richard Weston, *Modernism* (London: Phaidon, 1996).

Chapter 1: Introduction

Reyner Banham, *Guide to Modern Architecture* (Princeton, NJ: Van Nostrand, 1962).
Reyner Banham, *Theory and Design in the First Machine Age* (Cambridge, MA: MIT Press, 1980; first published 1960).
Zygmunt Bauman, *Liquid Modernity* (London: Polity, 2000).
Marshall Berman, *All That is Solid Melts into Air: The Experience of Modernity* (London: Verso, 2010).
Nathaniel Coleman, *Utopias and Architecture* (London: Routledge, 2005).
Le Corbusier, *Toward an Architecture*, trans. John Goodman (New York: Francis Lincoln, 2008; first published 1923 as *Vers Une Architecture*; first translated to English, 1927, as *Towards a New Architecture*).
William Curtis, *Modern Architecture Since 1900* (London: Phaidon, 1996).
Elizabeth Darling, *Re-forming Britain: Narratives of Modernity Before Reconstruction* (London: Routledge, 2007).

Sigfried Giedion, *Space, Time and Architecture: The Growth of a New Tradition* (Cambridge, MA: Harvard University Press, 2009; first published 1941).

Stuart Hall and Bram Gieben (eds), *Formations of Modernity* (London: Polity, 1992).

Michael Levenson (ed.), *The Cambridge Companion to Modernism* (Cambridge: Cambridge University Press, 2006).

Mary McLeod, 'Modernism', in Iain Borden, Murray Fraser, and Barbara Penner (eds), *Forty Ways to Think About Architecture: Architectural History and Theory Today* (London: Wiley, 2014), pp. 185–92.

Detlef Mertins, *Modernity Unbound: Other Histories of Architectural Modernity* (London: AA, 2014).

Nikolaus Pevsner, *An Outline of European Architecture* (Harmondsworth: Penguin, 1970; first published 1949).

Nikolaus Pevsner, *The Pioneers of Modern Design: From William Morris to Walter Gropius* (London: Penguin, 1991; first published 1936).

Henry Russell-Hitchcock and Philip Johnson, *The International Style* (New York: W.W. Norton & Co., 1997; first published 1932).

Manfredo Tafuri and Francesco Dal Co, *Modern Architecture* (New York: HH Abrams, 1979).

Giorgio Vasari, *The Lives of the Artists* (Oxford: Oxford University Press, 1991; first published 1550).

Robert Venturi, *Complexity and Contradiction in Architecture* (New York: MoMA, 1984; first published 1966).

Otto Wagner, *Modern Architecture*, ed. and trans. Harry Francis Mallgrave (Los Angeles: Getty Books, 1988; first published 1896).

Nigel Whiteley, *Reyner Banham: Historian of the Immediate Future* (Cambridge, MA: MIT Press, 2001).

Richard Saul Wurman (ed.), *What Will Be Has Always Been: The Words of Louis I. Kahn* (London: Rizzoli, 1986).

Chapter 2: Iron and steel

Rolf Achilles, *The Chicago School of Architecture: Building the Modern City, 1880–1910* (London: Shire Boooks, 2013).

Walter Benjamin, *The Arcades Project* (Cambridge, MA: Harvard University Press, 1999; written between 1927 and 1940, posthumously collected and edited).

Barry Bergdoll and Jennifer Gray, *Frank Lloyd Wright: Unpacking the Archive* (New York: MoMA, 2017).

Antony Bird, *Paxton's Palace* (London: Cassel, 1976).

H. Allen Brooks and Vincent Scully (eds), *The Prairie School: Frank Lloyd Wright and His Midwest Contemporaries* (New York, W.W. Norton, 2006).

Jean-Louis Cohen, *Mies van der Rohe* (Basel: Birkhäuser, 2011).

Jean-Louis Cohen and Christina Lodder, *Building the Revolution: Soviet Art and Architecture 1915–1935* (London: Royal Academy of Arts, 2011).

Kathleen James-Chakroborty (ed.), *Bauhaus Culture: From Weimar to the Cold War* (Minneapolis: University of Minnesota Press, 2006).

Robert Fishman, *Urban Utopias in the Twentieth Century* (Cambridge, MA: MIT Press, 1982).

Adrian Forty, 'Space', *Words and Buildings: A Vocabulary of Modern Architecture* (London: Thames and Hudson, 2000), pp. 256–75.

Sigfried Giedion, *Walter Gropius* (New York: Dover, 1993).

Joseph Harriss, *The Eiffel Tower: Symbol of an Age* (London: Paul Elek, 1976).

Margaret C. Jacob, *The Cultural Meaning of the Scientific Revolution* (New York: Alfred A. Knopf, 1988).

Mervyn D. Kaufman, *Father of Skyscrapers: A Biography of Louis Sullivan* (Boston: Little, Brown and Co., 1969).

Phyllis Lambert (ed.), *Mies in America* (New York: H.N. Abrams, 2001).

Neil Levine, 'The Romantic Idea of Architectural Legibility: Henri Labrouste and the Neo-Grec', in Arthur Drexler (ed.), *The Architecture of the Ecole des Beaux-Arts* (New York: MoMA, 1977), pp. 325–416.

Neil Levine, 'The Book and the Building: Hugo's Theory of Architecture and Labrouste's Bibliothèque Ste-Geneviève', in Robin Middleton (ed.), *The Beaux-Arts and Nineteenth Century French Architecture* (London: Thames and Hudson, 1982), pp. 138–73.

Christina Lodder, *Russian Constructivism* (New Haven: Yale, 1983).

Kevin Lynch, *Image of the City* (Cambridge, MA: MIT Press, 1960).

Harry Francis Mallgrave, *Gottfried Semper: Architect of the Nineteenth Century* (New Haven: Yale University Press, 1996).

Harry Francis Mallgrave, *Modern Architectural Theory: A Historical Survey, 1963–1968* (Cambridge: Cambridge University Press, 2005).

Robert McCarter, *Frank Lloyd Wright* (London: Phaidon, 1999).

James E. McClellan and Harold Dorn, *Science and Technology in World History: An Introduction* (Baltimore: Johns Hopkins University Press, 2006).

John McKean, *The Crystal Palace* (London: Phaidon, 1994).

Detlef Mertins, *Mies* (London: Phaidon, 2014).

Detlef Mertins, 'The Tectonic Unconscious', in *Modernity Unbound: Other Histories of Architectural Modernity* (London: AA, 2014), pp. 114–37.

John Milner, *Vladimir Tatlin and the Russian Avant-Garde* (New Haven: Yale University Press, 1983).

Hugh Morrison, *Louis Sullivan: Prophet of Modern Architecture* (New York: W.W. Norton, 1935).

Juliet Odgers, Mhairi McVicar, and Stephen Kite (eds), *Economy in Architecture* (London: Routledge, 2015).

Colin Rowe, 'Chicago Frame: Chicago's Place in the Modern Movement', *Architectural Review*, 120 (November 1956), 285–9.

Colin Rowe and Fred Slutsky, 'Transparency: Literal or Phenomenal', *Perspecta*, 8 (1963), 45–54.

Andrew Saint, *Architect and Engineer: A Study in Sibling Rivalry* (New Haven: Yale University Press, 2008).

Franz Schulze and Edward Windhorst, *Mies van der Rohe: A Critical Biography* (Chicago: University of Chicago Press, 2014).

Mitchell W. Schwarzer, 'The Emergence of Architectural Space: August Schmarsow's Theory of "Raumgestaltung"', *Assemblage*, 15 (1991), 48–61.

Philippe Sers, *Kandinsky: The Elements of Art* (London: Thames and Hudson, 2016).

Louis Sullivan, 'The Tall Office Building Artistically Considered', *Lippincott's Magazine*, 339 (March 1896), 403–9, <https://archive.org/details/tallofficebuildi00sull> (accessed 14 October 2017).

Ida van Zihl, *Gerrit Rietveld* (London: Phaidon, 2016).

Anthony Vidler, *Histories of the Immediate Present: Inventing Architectural Modernism* (Cambridge, MA: MIT Press, 2008).

Chapter 3: Reinforced concrete

Graham Allen, *Intertextuality* (London: Routledge, 2011).

Elisabeta Andreoli and Adrian Forty, *Brazil's Modern Architecture* (London: Phaidon, 2004).

Reyner Banham, *The New Brutalism: Ethic or Aesthetic?* (London: Architectural Press, 1966).

Tim Benton et al., *Le Corbusier: Architect of the Century* (London: Arts Council of Great Britain, 1987).

Federico Bucci, *Albert Kahn: Architect of Ford* (New Haven: Princeton Architectural Press, 2002).

Victor Buchli, 'Mosei Ginzburg's Narkomfin Communal House in Moscow: Contesting the Social and Material World', *Journal of the Society of Architectural Historians*, 57:2 (1998), 160–81.

Barnabus Calder, *Raw Concrete: The Beauty of Brutalism* (London: William Heinemann, 2016).

Frédéric Chaubin, *CCCP: Cosmic Communist Constructions Photographed* (Cologne: Taschen, 2011).

Jean-Louis Cohen, *Ludwig Mies van der Rohe* (Basel: Birkhäuser, 2018).

Beatriz Colomina, 'Battle Lines: E.1027', *Renaissance and Modern Studies*, 36:1 (1996), 95–105.

Caroline Constant, *Eileen Gray* (London: Phaidon, 2000).

Le Corbusier, *The Radiant City: Elements of a Doctrine of Urbanism to be Used as the Basis of our Machine-Age Civilisation* (London: Faber, 1967; 1st French edn, 1933).

Le Corbusier, *Toward an Architecture*, trans. John Goodman (London: Frances Lincoln, 2008; 1st edn in French, 1923; in English, 1927).

William Curtis, *Le Corbusier: Ideas and Forms* (London: Phaidon, 2015).

Gwenaël Delhumeau, 'La Maison en ciment armé de François Hennebique a Bourg-la-Reine', *Histoire de l'Art*, 9–10 May 1990.

Gabrel Feld et al., *Free University Berlin: Candilis, Josic, Woods, Schielhelm* (London: Architectural Association, 1999).

Adrian Forty, *Concrete and Culture: A Material History* (London: Reaktion, 2012).

Sigfried Giedeon, *Space, Time and Architecture: The Growth of a New Tradition* (Cambridge, MA: Harvard University Press, 1941).

Stephen Graham, *Vertical: The City from Satellites to Bunkers* (London: Verso, 2016).

Manuel Herz, Ingrid Schröder, Hans Focketyn, and Julia Jamrozik, *African Modernism: The Architecture of Independence—Ghana, Senegal, Côte d'Ivoire, Kenya, Zambia* (Zurich: Park Books, 2015).

Ben Highmore, *The Art of Brutalism: Rescuing Hope from Catastrophe in 1950s Britain* (New Haven: Yale University Press, 2017).

Charles Jencks, *Le Corbusier and the Tragic View of Architecture* (Cambridge, MA: Harvard University Press, 1973).

Seng Kuan and Yukio Lippit (eds), *Kenzō Tange: Architecture for the World* (Basel: Lars Müller, 2012).

Zhongjie Lin, *Kenzō Tange and the Metabolist Movement: Urban Utopias of Modern Japan* (London: Routledge, 2010).

Stanislaus von Moos et al., *Le Corbusier: The Art of Architecture* (Weil-am-Rhein, Vitra Design Museum, 2007).

Stephen Parnell, 'The Brutal Myth', *Thresholds*, 45 (2017), 152–60.

Styliane Phillipou, *Oscar Niemeyer: Curves of Irreverence* (New Haven: Yale University Press, 2008).

Michael Raeburn and Victoria Wilson (eds), *Le Corbusier: Architect of the Century* (London: Arts Council, 1987).

Max Risselada and Dirk van der Heuvel (eds), *Alison and Peter Smithson: A Critical Anthology* (Barcelona: Ediciones Poligrafa, 2011).

Katharina Ritter, Ekaterina Shapiro-Obermair, Dietmar Steiner, and Alexandra Wachter, *Soviet Modernism 1955–1991* (Vienna and Zurich: Architekturzentrum and Park Books, 2012).

Moshe Safdie, *Beyond Habitat by 20 Years* (Toronto: Tundra Books, 1986).

Flora Samuel, *Le Corbusier in Detail* (London: Architectural Press, 2007).

Flora Samuel and Inge Linder-Gaillard, *Sacred Concrete: The Churches of Le Corbusier* (Basel: Birkhäuser, 2013).

Claire Zimmerman, 'The Labor of Albert Kahn', <http://www.we-aggregate.org/> (accessed 14 October 2017).

Chapter 4: Brick

Janne Ahlin, *Sigurd Lewerentz, Architect: 1885–1975* (Zurich: Park Books, 2014).

Benedict Anderson, *Imagined Communities: Reflections on the Origin and Spread of Nationalism* (London: Verso, 2006).

Peter Blundell Jones, *Hugo Häring: The Organic Versus the Geometric* (Stuttgart: Axel Menges, 2002).

David Brownlee and David De Long, *Louis I. Kahn: In the Realm of Architecture* (London: Thames and Hudson, 2005).

Harry Charrington and Vezio Nuva, *Alvar Aalto: The Mark of the Hand* (Helsinki: Rakennustieto, 2011).

Nathaniel Coleman, *Utopias and Architecture* (London: Routledge, 2005).

Kenneth Frampton, 'Towards a Critical Regionalism: Six Points for an Architecture of Resistance', in Hal Foster (ed.), *The Anti-Aesthetic: Essays on Postmodern Culture* (Seattle: Bay Press, 1983).

Neil Levine, 'The Aesthetic of the Unfinished and the Example of Louis I. Kahn', in *Modern Architecture: Representation and Reality* (New Haven: Yale University Press, 2009).

Michael Lewis et al., *Louis Kahn: The Power of Architecture* (Weil-am-Rhein: Vitra Design Museum, 2013).

John Lobell, *Between Silence and Light: Spirit in the Architecture of Louis I. Kahn* (Boulder, CO: Shambhala Publications, 2008).

Robert McCarter, *Louis I. Kahn* (London: Phaidon, 2009).

Annie Pedret, *Team 10: An Archival History* (London: Routledge, 2013).

Max Risselada and Dirk van den Heuvel, *Team 10: 1953–81, in Search of a Utopia of the Present* (Rotterdam: NAi, 2005).

Göran Schildt, *Alvar Aalto in His Own Words* (Helsinki: Otava, 1997).

Vincent Scully, 'Louis I. Kahn and the Ruins of Rome', *Engineering and Science*, Winter (1993), 3–13.

Alison Smithson, *Team 10 Primer* (Cambridge, MA: MIT Press, 1974).

Wilfried Wang, *St. Petri, Sigurd Lewerentz* (Tübingen: Ernst Wasmuth, 2009).

Richard Weston, *Town Hall, Saynatsalo 1951, Alvar Aalto* (London: Phaidon, 1993).

Richard Weston, *Alvar Aalto* (London: Phaidon, 1995).

Sarah Williams Goldhagen, *Louis Kahn's Situated Modernism* (New Haven: Yale University Press, 2001).

Sarah Williams Goldhagen and Rejean Legault (eds), *Anxious Modernisms: Experimentation in Postwar Architectural Culture* (Cambridge, MA: MIT Press, 2001).

Colin St John Wilson, *The Other Tradition of Modern Architecture: The Uncompleted Project* (London: Academy Editions, 1995).

Chapter 5: Light and air

Donald Albrecht and Eeva-Liisa Pelknonen, *Eero Saarinen: Shaping the Future* (New Haven: Yale University Press, 2011).

Jean Baudrillard, 'The Beaubourg-Effect: Implosion and Deterrence', *October*, 20 (Spring, 1982), 3–13.

Peter Buchanan, *Renzo Piano Building Workshop: Complete Works* Vol. 1 (London: Phaidon, 1993).

Manuel Castells, *The Rise of the Network Society* (London: Wiley, 1996).

Francesco Dal Co, *Centre Pompidou: Renzo Piano, Richard Rogers and the Making of a Modern Monument* (New Haven: Yale University Press, 2016).

Jonathan Hughes and Simon Sadler (eds), *Non Plan: Essays on Freedom, Participation and Change in Modern Architecture and Urbanism* (London: Routledge, 1999).

Jane Jacobs, *The Death and Life of Great American Cities* (New York: Random House, 2011; 1st edn 1961).

David Jenkins (ed.), *Norman Foster: Works 1* (New York: Prestel, 2003).

Caroline Maniaque-Benton and Meredith Gaglio, *Whole Earth Field Guide* (Cambridge, MA: MIT Press, 2016).

Reinhold Martin, *The Organizational Complex* (Cambridge, MA: MIT Press, 1995).

Arthur Marwick, *The Sixties: Social and Cultural Transformation in Britain, France, Italy and the United States, 1958–74* (Oxford: Oxford University Press, 1999).

James Meller (ed.), *Buckminster Fuller Reader* (London: Jonathan Cape, 1970).

Jayne Merkel, *Eero Saarinen* (London: Phaidon, 2014).

Martin Pawley, *Buckminster Fuller* (Miami: Taplinger, 1990).

Kenneth Powell, *Richard Rogers: Complete Works*, Vol. 1 (London: Phaidon, 1999).

Simon Sadler, *Archigram: Architecture Without Architecture* (Cambridge, MA: MIT Press, 2003).

Felicity Scott, *Architecture or Techno-Utopia: Politics after Modernism* (Cambridge, MA: MIT Press, 2007).

Felicity Scott, *Ant Farm: Living Architecture 7* (Barcelona: Actar, 2008).

Lloyd Stephen Seiden, *Buckminster Fuller's Universe* (New York: Basic, 1989).

Mark Wigley, *Buckminster Fuller Inc.: Architecture in the Age of Radio* (Baden: Lars Müller, 2015).

Chapter 6: Conclusion

Marshall Berman, *All That is Solid Melts into Air: The Experience of Modernity* (London: Verso, 2010).

Allison Dutoit, Juliet Odgers, and Adam Sharr (eds), *Quality Out of Control: Standards for Measuring Architecture* (London: Routledge, 2010).

Terry Farrell and Adam Nathaniel Furman, *Revisiting Postmodernism* (London: RIBA, 2017).

Roberto Gargiani, *Rem Koolhaas | OMA* (London: Routledge, 2008).

Diane Ghirado, *Architecture After Modernism* (London: Thames and Hudson, 1996).

Anthony Giddens, *The Consequences of Modernity* (Stanford: Stanford University Press, 1990).

Elijah Huge and Stephanie Tuerk, *Perspecta 35: Building Codes* (Cambridge, MA: MIT Press, 2004).

Rob Imrie and Emma Street, *Architectural Design and Regulation* (London: Wiley-Blackwell, 2011).

Charles Jencks, *The Language of Post-Modern Architecture* (London: Academy Editions, 1977).

Charles Jencks, *The Story of Postmodernism: Five Decades of the Ironic, Iconic and Critical in Architecture* (London: John Wiley, 2011).

Diébédo Francis Kéré, Andres Lepik, and Ayça Beygo, *Francis Kéré: Radically Simple* (Stuttgart: Hatje Cantz, 2017).

Rem Koolhaas, 'Miestakes', in *New Materiality: A+T 23* (Vitoria Gasteiz: A+T, 2004).

Léon Krier, *Léon Krier: Architecture and Urban Design*, ed. Richard Economakis (London: Academy Editions, 1992).

Katie Lloyd Thomas, Tilo Amhoff, and Nick Beech (eds), *Industries of Architecture* (London: Routledge, 2016).

Matthew Poole and Manuel Schvartzberg (eds), *The Politics of Parametricism: Digital Technologies in Architecture* (London: Bloomsbury, 2015).

Wang Shu, *Wang Shu and Amateur Architecture Studio* (Basel: Lars Müller, 2017).

Further reading

I've examined buildings in this book—and ideas informing them—which proved so inspirational or troubling that their organization and imagery helped shape modern architecture. I've tried to emphasize *what* modern architecture was like, *why* it was like that, and *how* it was imagined, more than global patterns of *where* and *when*. Jean-Louis Cohen's introduction to modern architecture, *The Future of Architecture Since 1899* (London: Phaidon, 2012) is a counterweight to mine. It catalogues a vast diversity of modern buildings into periods and movements across an impressive geographical range, emphasizing the *where* and *when*, although it seldom addresses individual buildings in detail. It'll help you identify distinctive cultures of modern architecture near you.

The vocabulary of modern architecture, and its influence over buildings and architectural cultures, is explored in Adrian Forty's *Words and Buildings* (London: Thames and Hudson, 2004). Richard Weston's *Modernism* (London: Phaidon, 1995) accounts for the emergence of prewar modern architecture in relation to broader movements in art and culture. Meanwhile, *Anxious Modernisms: Experimentation in Postwar Architectural Culture* (Cambridge, MA: MIT Press, 2001), edited by Sarah Williams Goldhagen and Rejean Legault, scopes-out diverse postwar approaches.

Architectural theories

Throughout the period of modernity, a body of architectural theory writing set out to contest and consolidate modern architecture's values. Harry Francis Mallgrave's *Modern Architectural Theory: A Historical Survey, 1673–1968* (Cambridge: Cambridge University Press, 2005) sets that theory in a longer historical context. Alongside Corbusier's *Towards an Architecture*, Pevsner's *Pioneers of Modern Design*, Giedeon's *Space, Time and Architecture*, and *The International Style* catalogue, three further key texts outlined the contours of modern architectural theory: Lewis Mumford's *Technics and Civilisation* (New York: Harcourt Brace, 1934); Bruno Zevi's *Architecture as Space: How to Look at Architecture* (New York: Horizon Press, 1957; 1st Italian edn, 1948); and Manfredo Tafuri's *Theories and History of Architecture* (London: Academy Editions, 1980; 1st Italian edn, 1968).

Two anthologies have collected together influential 20th-century architectural theory essays making polemical claims about the future. Charles Jencks and Karl Kropf edited *Theories and Manifestoes of Contemporary Architecture*, which illustrates vividly the zeal of the essay writers (London: John Wiley, 2005; 1st edn, 1997). Jonathan A. Hale and William Braham's *Rethinking Technology: A Reader in Architectural Theory* (London: Routledge, 2007), meanwhile, collects architects' reflections on the technologies that shaped modern architecture.

Global modern architectures

There's a growing—and much needed—English language literature on modern architectures beyond Europe and the Anglosphere. *African Modernism* by Manuel Herz (Zurich: Park Books, 2015) explores work in Ghana, Senegal, Ivory Coast, Kenya, and Zambia. Its excellent introduction surveys questions of colonial and postcolonial modern architectures in Africa and beyond. *Modernism in China: Architectural Visions and Revolutions* (London: Wiley, 2008), by Edward Denison, accounts for early modern architecture in that country in relation to its particular experiences of modernity. Jianfei Zhu's *Architecture of Modern China: A Critique* (London: Routledge, 2008) has a longer reach, from 1729 to 2008, although focusing primarily on the 20th century, specifically from the Maoist period to the foundations of present professional practice.

David B. Stewart's *The Making of a Modern Japanese Architecture: From the Founders to Shinohara and Isozaki* (New York: Kodansha

America, 1988) locates modern architecture in the rise, defeat, and rebirth of contemporary Japan.

Meanwhile, Luis E. Carranza and Fernando Luiz Lara's *Modern Architecture in Latin America: Art, Technology and Utopia* (Austin: University of Texas Press, 2015) thoughtfully introduces ideas and projects in various countries and contexts.

Using and abusing architectural history

Where architectural historians and critics have usually preferred to categorize and interpret buildings, practising architects tend to tap history for examples relevant to their present work. Modern architects called this precedent study—inspired by J.N.L. Durand's 18th-century architectural analyses, and D'Arcy Wentworth Thompson's studies of growth and form in nature—and they had no problem plundering examples from diverse periods and cultures for tactics to organize space. Historian Manfredo Tafuri was sceptical of this approach—see *Theories and History of Architecture* mentioned earlier—calling it 'operative criticism', recognizing how it tends to impose contemporary priorities on the past, neglecting architecture's broader cultural consequences. A helpful account of divergent approaches to modern, and present-day, architectural history—and their abuses by architects, historians, and critics—can be found in Andrew Leach's *What is Architectural History?* (London: Polity, 2010). *The Historiography of Modern Architecture* by Panayotis Tournikotis (Cambridge, MA: MIT Press, 2001), meanwhile, highlights how the histories of modern architecture mostly got written from their own present. Lastly, if my approach in this book appeals to you—reading buildings for their insights into the cultures and individuals who procured, constructed, and inhabited them—then I make a shameless plug for my own edited collection on architectural research methods: *Reading Architecture and Culture: Researching Buildings, Spaces and Documents* (London: Routledge, 2012).

Index

Page numbers in italics refer to photographs.

Index

GLOBALIZATION
A Very Short Introduction
Manfred Steger

'Globalization' has become one of the defining buzzwords of our time - a term that describes a variety of accelerating economic, political, cultural, ideological, and environmental processes that are rapidly altering our experience of the world. It is by its nature a dynamic topic - and this *Very Short Introduction* has been fully updated for 2009, to include developments in global politics, the impact of terrorism, and environmental issues. Presenting globalization in accessible language as a multifaceted process encompassing global, regional, and local aspects of social life, Manfred B. Steger looks at its causes and effects, examines whether it is a new phenomenon, and explores the question of whether, ultimately, globalization is a good or a bad thing.

www.oup.com/vsi

CHAOS
A Very Short Introduction
Leonard Smith

Our growing understanding of Chaos Theory is having fascinating applications in the real world - from technology to global warming, politics, human behaviour, and even gambling on the stock market. Leonard Smith shows that we all have an intuitive understanding of chaotic systems. He uses accessible maths and physics (replacing complex equations with simple examples like pendulums, railway lines, and tossing coins) to explain the theory, and points to numerous examples in philosophy and literature (Edgar Allen Poe, Chang-Tzu, Arthur Conan Doyle) that illuminate the problems. The beauty of fractal patterns and their relation to chaos, as well as the history of chaos, and its uses in the real world and implications for the philosophy of science are all discussed in this *Very Short Introduction*.

'. . . Chaos . . . will give you the clearest (but not too painful idea) of the maths involved . . . There's a lot packed into this little book, and for such a technical exploration it's surprisingly readable and enjoyable - I really wanted to keep turning the pages. Smith also has some excellent words of wisdom about common misunderstandings of chaos theory . . .'

popularscience.co.uk

www.oup.com/vsi

DIPLOMACY
A Very Short Introduction
Joseph M. Siracusa

Like making war, diplomacy has been around a very long time, at least since the Bronze Age. It was primitive by today's standards, there were few rules, but it was a recognizable form of diplomacy. Since then, diplomacy has evolved greatly, coming to mean different things, to different persons, at different times, ranging from the elegant to the inelegant. Whatever one's definition, few could doubt that the course and consequences of the major events of modern international diplomacy have shaped and changed the global world in which we live. Joseph M. Siracusa introduces the subject of diplomacy from a historical perspective, providing examples from significant historical phases and episodes to illustrate the art of diplomacy in action.

'Professor Siracusa provides a lively introduction to diplomacy through the perspective of history.'

Gerry Woodard, Senior Fellow in Political Science at the University of Melbourne and former Australasian Ambassador in Asia

Economics
A Very Short Introduction
Partha Dasgupta

Economics has the capacity to offer us deep insights into
some of the most formidable problems of life, and offer
solutions to them too. Combining a global approach with
examples from everyday life, Partha Dasgupta describes the
lives of two children who live very different lives in different
parts of the world: in the Mid-West USA and in Ethiopia. He
compares the obstacles facing them, and the processes that
shape their lives, their families, and their futures. He shows
how economics uncovers these processes, finds explanations
for them, and how it forms policies and solutions.

'An excellent introduction . . . presents mathematical and statistical
findings in straightforward prose.'

Financial Times

www.oup.com/vsi

FREE SPEECH
A Very Short Introduction
Nigel Warburton

'I disapprove of what you say, but I will defend to the death your right to say it' This slogan, attributed to Voltaire, is frequently quoted by defenders of free speech. Yet it is rare to find anyone prepared to defend all expression in every circumstance, especially if the views expressed incite violence. So where do the limits lie? What is the real value of free speech? Here, Nigel Warburton offers a concise guide to important questions facing modern society about the value and limits of free speech: Where should a civilized society draw the line? Should we be free to offend other people's religion? Are there good grounds for censoring pornography? Has the Internet changed everything? This Very Short Introduction is a thought-provoking, accessible, and up-to-date examination of the liberal assumption that free speech is worth preserving at any cost.

'The genius of Nigel Warburton's *Free Speech* lies not only in its extraordinary clarity and incisiveness. Just as important is the way Warburton addresses freedom of speech - and attempts to stifle it - as an issue for the 21st century. More than ever, we need this book.'

Denis Dutton, University of Canterbury, New Zealand

www.oup.com/vsi

FORENSIC SCIENCE
A Very Short Introduction
Jim Fraser

In this Very Short Introduction, Jim Fraser introduces the concept of forensic science and explains how it is used in the investigation of crime. He begins at the crime scene itself, explaining the principles and processes of crime scene management. He explores how forensic scientists work; from the reconstruction of events to laboratory examinations. He considers the techniques they use, such as fingerprinting, and goes on to highlight the immense impact DNA profiling has had. Providing examples from forensic science cases in the UK, US, and other countries, he considers the techniques and challenges faced around the world.

An admirable alternative to the 'CSI' science fiction juggernaut...Fascinating.

William Darragh, Fortean Times

www.oup.com/vsi

GEOPOLITICS
A Very Short Introduction
Klaus Dodds

In certain places such as Iraq or Lebanon, moving a few
feet either side of a territorial boundary can be a matter of life
or death, dramatically highlighting the connections between
place and politics. For a country's location and size as well as
its sovereignty and resources all affect how the people that live
there understand and interact with the wider world. Using
wide-ranging examples, from historical maps to James Bond
films and the rhetoric of political leaders like Churchill and
George W. Bush, this Very Short Introduction shows why,
for a full understanding of contemporary global politics, it is
not just smart - it is essential - to be geopolitical.

'Engrossing study of a complex topic.'

Mick Herron, Geographical.

www.oup.com/vsi